# MOM'S DIARY

## A Story of Loss, Reflection, and Hope

# MICHAEL WEST

For rights and permissions, please contact:

Michael R. West
320 Corporate Drive
Knoxville, Tennessee 37923

Michael.west864@gmail.com

Paperback ISBN: 979-8-9894753-0-8
Hardcover ISBN: 979-8-9894753-1-5
eBook ISBN: 979-8-9894753-2-2

Cover design and typesetting by: riverdesignbooks.com

*To mom, dad, and Rick for the gift of family and their love that defined and sustained me.*

# INTRODUCTION

I DIDN'T KNOW WHERE TO PUT IT. Should I store it away, out of sight and out of mind? That was the safest thing for me. If I tucked it in a box, maybe I would never see it again, feel drawn to read it and risk the chance of learning something I couldn't handle. Or maybe I could give it a prominent placement in the house. Something not obvious to others, but noticeable to me. It would be easy to do. Even an uncluttered house has small items lying around that go unnoticed. It ended up in my home office—the room where I spend so much time.

I love to read—the feeling of a book, the satisfaction of placing it on the shelf when it has shared its story with me, the fun of organizing it with similar books, and the chance, at some future date, to consider its words.

Because I'm never willing to end my relationship with a good book, I catalog titles together by theme or topic.

It's fun to spend time thinking about where a book should rest—part of my connection to the moment, hopefully for a long time to come.

Mom's diary didn't fit anywhere for me. Unlike all the other books in my small library, this one was deeply personal. I didn't know for sure, but she likely wrote things about me. What did she write? How did I disappoint her? Did she have secrets that should remain secret? Most importantly, did she ever think I'd possess this and read it someday? Damn, how was I supposed to know any of this? I realized that hidden within its pages was a story I doubted I wanted to revisit. Not knowing what it said was terrifying. How could I give it a place in a room alongside books I'd read and chronicled for future reflection?

The process of determining in what section it belonged on my shelves was haphazard. I tried to figure out logically where I wanted it to reside but couldn't make sense of it. I didn't want it to be obvious to me when I sat in any of the chairs in the room. After all, I didn't want to see it. Even though I wasn't storing it in a box in the attic, I was trying to hide it in plain sight. If my avoidance was to be complete, it needed to be placed in a section I was unlikely to frequent. With these parameters in mind, the diary found itself tucked away with reference books, beside a dictionary, thesaurus, a book on wine tasting, a guide to preparing for a marathon, and a few Bibles—all genres that I was unlikely to want or need.

It's been more than 20 years since dad gave me a shoebox full of mom's personal items that included her diary. I don't know whether dad knew the box's contents, and if he did, whether he ever read the diary. He never said, I never asked, and so we existed with an unspoken secret. I assume that he didn't read it.

As for me, over a two-decade period, I picked up the diary three times. Each time, I was moved to grab it due to some emotional memory. I turned to a random page with a random entry and began to read, and every time, I stopped before completing a passage. The writing was raw, emotional, and so personal, I was unable to continue. There wasn't a particular statement or insight that caused me to recoil. I just wasn't prepared or emotionally ready for what was memorialized. Three times in 20 years. Long intervals between all three attempts numbed me to the point that I didn't retain anything that I had previously read. I just remember feeling panic and pain.

Over the past few days, I've found myself staring blankly at the diary—drawn to it in ways that are unfamiliar to me. It's important that I connect with mom, even if it's painful. I began to wonder: Will this be exclusively a traumatic journey? Mom was a cheerfully happy person—smiling, laughing, teasing people, and telling stories while loving those in her orbit passionately. I assume that a person who lived cheerfully also would express joy privately. I so desperately hope that's true. I'm prepared to ingest the suffering I know I'll find in her words. I also want to feel her loving presence. She laughed all the time. I'd like to laugh when I read her words. Maybe it's too much to ask. I don't know. There's so much I don't know.

I've been writing a book about mom in my head for five years. In that time, I've gotten closer to understanding how intertwined my life was, and is, with mom's, how her fight with cancer altered me and how inadequate I was at being there for her. And yet, I also have grown to understand how her struggles, toughness, and love were, and are, always inside of me. She lives within my soul, and I'm learning to accept that even though she isn't here and I can't talk to her, I can live my life my way, which was what she always wanted: to live her life her way.

So here I am––her diary on my desk––feeling apprehensive, excited, and tearful––but I think I'm ready. It's time for me to read her words. I want my written words to be a tribute to hers. Admittedly, I don't even know what that means, but I intend to honor what she writes and, I hope, process it as best I can. The first entry is dated August 13, 1992: "*Surgery*."

# PART I

# CHAPTER 1

Mom's dad, Thomas Hudson Knight was born into extreme poverty on March 9, 1917. The eighth child of nine, born to Thomas Knight and Nora Jinks, Tommy likely never had a chance to grow out of his economic circumstances. His father would die months after Tommy turned 10. His mother did whatever she could to provide for her children, and it was barely enough. Ultimately, three of the nine would die before becoming adults. When Tommy was 12, the stock market crashed, and the nation soon sank into the Great Depression. For a family that was barely getting by, bad got worse. Tommy spent his teenage years struggling to survive the Depression, so for him, school was secondary to survival. Thus, he didn't get his high school diploma. Like so many men of his era, World War II military service offered a chance at a better future.

After the war began, Tommy enlisted in the US Army Air Force, expecting to fight for his country—a reasonable assumption. For most enlisted men, unless you joined the military with a clearly defined skill that contributed to supporting the war effort, combat was likely. That's what Tommy expected. But fighting wasn't in his future. He was assigned to work as a baker, charged with creating desserts for officers and their staff. Tommy never knew why he was given this role. He received his orders, and he followed them. Admittedly, baking for the brass wasn't a critical task, but he was good at it and quickly discovered that he had a gift: decorating cakes. How he discovered this talent or where it came from was a mystery to his family. He never talked about it, so the transition from hardscrabble Depression-era teenager without a skill to a talented baker who had a craft and a future livelihood after the war is a piece of his history that we'll never know. Initially, he was stationed at the Army Air Force base in Smyrna, Tennessee. While stationed here, he met his future wife, Margie Estelle Warren. Estelle was young and naïve.

Born July 31, 1926, Estelle was nine years younger than Tommy. Estelle's dad, Jesse James Warren, was a tenant farmer. Her mother, Kim Davis Heath, gave birth to 11 kids, Estelle being the sixth. Without birth control, having lots of kids wasn't uncommon. They also needed kids to work. In this case, the Warrens required a large family to work on the farm they were living on. Tenant farming provided few opportunities and a limited future. It was hard living, and Estelle's family survived the Depression plowing someone else's fields. When the kids were old enough, they started working. Working the land didn't allow for schooling. Estelle finished 11th grade and, like her siblings, went to work. She recalled they were always moving and once joked, "We must've lived on almost every farm in Rutherford County."

The war didn't change the Warrens' outlook. In fact, life was harder. Those who weren't working in the fields were contributing to the war effort. The country was sacrificing to ensure victory, and the Warrens did their part. However, fewer family workers meant there was the same amount of work to do on the farm and fewer hands to do it.

Smyrna, Tennessee, and its airfield were in Rutherford County. Estelle worked on the base during her teenage years when she met Tommy. She should've been focusing on completing her education, but the draw of Tommy and a better life captivated her. Tommy was handsome, and in the eyes of Estelle, a worldly man who charmed her from the beginning. Estelle had never left Rutherford County. Tommy was from Knoxville, and he was scheduled to transfer to Hawaii.

As was customary during this era, their courtship was brief. Despite the hardships, Estelle had experienced a happy childhood, but was ready for a brighter future. Tommy also was anxious to build a better life, and Estelle was a beautiful young woman who offered a path to happier times. On January 26, 1945, in a little church in Murfreesboro, Tennessee, they were wed. Still a few months before the end of the war, they entered their covenant together excited about the future and ready to chart their own path. Nearly a year later, on January 7, 1946, my mom, Patricia Ann Knight, was born in a small, rented house on Detroit Avenue in Knoxville, Tennessee.

Their first home was a step up from life before they married, but it was a long way from their aspirational goals. They were proud people who knew how to work hard. They believed their future was theirs to control, and they quickly set about the task of providing a home and raising a daughter. However, the deck was stacked against them.

Before the war, a formal education had alluded Tommy, and thus, he didn't pursue a college education through the GI Bill. A free college education was a blessing offered by a grateful nation to those who had served. For millions of returning GIs, this was a big first step out of a bleak Depression-era life into a solidly middle-class future. Unfortunately, it was a missed opportunity for the newlyweds to pull themselves up the economic ladder. Not surprisingly, as the general population became more educated, a economic gap developed between them and those left behind. That's not to say that none of these people ever elevated their status and achieved a middle-class lifestyle. It just meant that the road was harder, and misfortune or bad luck could be devastating.

Tommy didn't have a degree, but he had a skill, and Max Wolf, a prominent community leader and owner of Quality Bakery, was eager to hire Tommy as a decorator of all things sweet. This was a respectable job working at a respected company. As Tommy settled into his role, Estelle went to work as a soda pop counter girl at a local drugstore. I can only imagine the smiles she brought to the customers she served. Always there to please, I'm sure she brought energy and love to the counter.

In a few short years, the couple saved enough to buy a little farmhouse in Bear Holler across the Tennessee River from downtown Knoxville. It wasn't much, but it was their home. Tommy kept his job at the bakery while Estelle began to raise a family. When mom was five, the family of three welcomed another girl, Karen, to the fold. Five years after Karen, Pam was added, and the family was complete. Three girls perfectly spaced, each five years apart––an interesting feat that Estelle didn't want to explain to Karen. When Karen asked how she was able to accomplish such a well-timed schedule, Estelle raised her eyebrows, glared disapprovingly at her, and grunted, "Really?" That was the end of the inquiry. A Southern girl wouldn't discuss certain things, no matter how interesting the subject.

Life on the farm wasn't an idyllic fantasy, but it represented the best of times for the Knight family. Three kids, a reliable job, and everyone was healthy. Days were spent raising chickens, doing daily chores, and playing in the woods. Mom being the oldest, it was her role to be the responsible one. Karen remembered Saturday as the day mom chose to wield her sibling power. Each Saturday, the girls were tasked with cleaning the house. As Karen tells it, mom made her younger sisters scrub the house from top to bottom.

Life was good, and the family settled into a comfortable 1950s existence. All seemed well, but it wasn't. Tommy was having stomach problems. Diagnosed with stomach ulcers, he was struggling with severe gastrointestinal pain. At the time, the medical community didn't understand the cause of ulcers, how to treat them, or even that curing an ulcer was possible. The doctors tried everything to alleviate the pain, but nothing worked. Eventually, a drastic decision was made that was viewed as the only hope: surgery to remove portions of his stomach and eliminate the affected area. As hard as it is to believe, the surgeon removed roughly three-fourths of his stomach. Today, doctors understand that a bacterium causes peptic ulcers and that antibiotics can be used to treat them. However, in the late 1950s, a scalpel was the course chosen, and the impact was disastrous and permanent.

Before the lasting physical effects of the misguided and botched surgery surfaced, another more obvious change resulted from the procedure. The Knights had to sell their home to pay for the surgery. All their hard work to get ahead was gone. They were starting over, and now the primary breadwinner was sick. The family moved back to a house on Detroit Avenue, renting from Tommy's cousin Ed, who was anything but supportive, showing little sympathy for his relative. Soon afterward, Tommy went back to work at Quality Bakery, as Max Wolf was there for him and the family. In fact, he registered them for a social program to help provide support for the struggling family. Tommy and Estelle were appreciative, but embarrassed. They didn't have much, but they had pride and were willing to work hard. Unfortunately, hard work wasn't enough. They didn't want a handout, but they needed it.

Help also came from Estelle's family. The year Tommy underwent his surgery, there was no money to give the girls Christmas presents. However, two of Estelle's older brothers, James and Robert, stepped in and played Santa. Mom and Karen found out what they did. It was an act that reinforced in the girls that family takes care of each other. That sweet gift lasted a lifetime as both mom and Karen carried the loving torch, taking care of others as part of their core beliefs.

Through perseverance and a strong sense of pride, Tommy and Estelle made it out of the renter's cycle and bought a cute three-bedroom house on Windsor Avenue, across from West High School. Sadly, Tommy was still sick, his stomach tiny and unable to hold much food. Worse yet, the doctors failed to cauterize the peptic nerve adequately, which meant Tommy's stomach continuously filled with acid, resulting in a cycle of him vomiting all day. Keeping food down was a challenge, and as such, a formerly healthy, strong man now weighed 120 pounds. Furthermore, complicating his health, Tommy smoked two packs a day, ultimately leading to emphysema. However, he didn't know this would become his fate. In fact, doctors during this era encouraged people to smoke. His doctors told him that smoking would calm his nerves and reduce the "stress induced" stomach ulcers.

Despite his illness, Tommy worked a few more years trying to provide for the family. However, by the early 1960s, it became too much, and he was deemed 100% disabled. This was a blow to Tommy, and he never fully recovered. By the grace of God, Estelle found work at Allied Chemical Corporation working on the factory floor sewing seat belts. It was a hard job, but it was a blessing.

Despite the family hardships, the girls flourished in the house on Windsor Avenue and enjoyed the benefits of local public schooling. Fortunately, West High zoning captured Windsor Avenue students, but it also included Sequoyah Hills, the most upscale part of Knoxville. West High was a good public school, providing an education to give the girls future opportunities. For Tommy and Estelle, it had been hard as hell, but they were giving their girls the chance they never had.

Mom was a better-than-average student who excelled at math and thrived at West High. I knew she was smart and heard her reflect on how much she loved school. That's why for me, all these years later, there was something missing from this story. Mom's younger sisters, Karen and Pam, went to college, and mom didn't. I always wondered about this, but sadly never asked her why. I eventually asked my Aunt Karen, "How come you and Pam went to college, and mom didn't?" Her answer floored me: "You know your mom had a scholarship to Sewanee." Shocked to hear this, I asked, "Why didn't she go?" There was a very long pause. "Do you really want to know?" she replied. "Of course," I said. "Your dad wouldn't let her go."

Tears filled my eyes as I began to process this. Of course he stopped her. It wasn't hard for me to believe.

# CHAPTER 2

**August 18, 1992**

*Came home from the hospital. Doctor gave me 15 Percocet for pain.*

**August 22, 1992**

*Returned to Dr. Vickers to check on tube and remove half of the staples. At this point, the tube in my side was killing me. The doctor gave me 12 Lorcet tablets for pain.*

P EOPLE TOLERATE PAIN DIFFERENTLY. RESEARCH has shown that there's both a biological and psychological aspect to how people feel pain, express their pain, and seek solutions to alleviate it. I had a friend whose dad's cancer was all over his body, and his doctors were certain that the tumors' intrusion into his bones and organs hurt badly. And yet, he never expressed feelings of pain, nor sought to relieve whatever discomfort he felt. And yet, I can recall times when I've seen people look like they're suffering the worst pain imaginable from a small cut.

When something happens to cause pain, the affected area signals the brain to let it know there's a problem. The brain then processes the newly identified concern and decides how to react. In some instances, the brain drives a person to move on and ignore what has caused the brain to be alerted. Other times, every activity or thought ceases as the body focuses on the injury and how to make it feel better.

In a WebMD article on pain management, Doris Cope, an anesthesiologist in the Pain Medicine Program at the University of Pittsburgh Medical Center, pointed out, "Pain is both a biochemical and neurological transmission of an unpleasant sensation and an emotional experience." Taken further, "Chronic pain actually changes the way the spinal cord, nerves, and brain process unpleasant stimuli, causing hypersensitization, but the brain and emotions can moderate or intensify the pain." Thus, our past, good and bad, influence how we feel pain.

This makes sense to me. For some, pain is part of living, while for others, pain becomes all consuming—the central theme of their lives. Mom's initial entries in her diary seemed harmless, but they rocked me. When I reflect on mom's fight against cancer, I always struggle to understand how pain medication became such a controlling aspect of her life.

In hindsight, we should've been better prepared for what was to come. When the diagnosis of breast cancer came down, mom was 46 and otherwise healthy, but her health hadn't always been good. Seven years earlier, she was diagnosed with adult cerebral vasculitis, a rare condition that was described at the time as something found after the patient had died from a stroke. The doctors didn't know what was going on, how to treat it, nor even if it could be treated. Their uncertainty scared the hell out of mom, and her anxiety naturally grew. Xanax was the perfect tonic for her rattled nerves.

I was out of the house and admittedly not well-informed about her condition's severity and uncertainty. I also was unaware of her growing fondness for Xanax.

Miraculously, in time, her condition and the frightening diagnosis faded. I honestly don't know whether the doctors got the original diagnosis right or not. Her doctors told her that she had a ticking time bomb in her head—something that should've killed her without her knowing she had it. She was given an aggressive cocktail of medications, including very high doses of Prednisone. In time, the doctors told her that tests revealed less danger, then after a few years, mom never talked about the disease, nor her fears of it. She was back to good health. I don't know if she stopped using Xanax.

Five days removed from a mastectomy must amplify the two aspects of pain. Biologically, it hurts, badly. Combine the searing pain with her history, and it's not surprising that she was focusing on her pain and how to fix it. For me, it's just sad. At the time, it never occurred to me that her pain, the need to stop it, and what she was taking would consume her and those around her. I don't know how we could've recognized the early signs of trouble. She was in pain, she was scared, and so were we.

Even though I'm reading her story for the first time. I know what's coming and what happened, at least through my own lens. However, until I opened her diary, I only could guess how she processed this journey. To be sure, I have no doubt she was in pain and that she needed pain medication. However, her immediate fixation on medication that could alter how she felt supports a pattern she continued for the remainder of her life.

Thirty years ago, dependence on pain medication wasn't discussed openly. Pain management wasn't viewed widely as a subspecialty. Some physicians were very hesitant to prescribe pain relief through narcotics, while others were less concerned with their lasting effects. In time, the medical community has gathered more knowledge about best practices for pain management. And yet, the US now faces an opioid epidemic that has rocked society across all demographic groups. What we now know is that some people are predisposed to addiction, and pain medications create a mainstream pathway to various dependencies that might not have been present in a person's normal life. I never thought of mom as having an addictive personality. Frankly, as a non-clinician, I wasn't a good judge of her vulnerability to addiction. Today, I remain a layman and, thus, still lack a background with which to draw a definitive conclusion.

However, I don't have to be an expert to know that

mom very quickly became dependent on medication. In her first diary entries she's singularly focused on her pain and a precise chronicling of what she was prescribed. As I write this, I feel I'm being harsh. Maybe I am, or maybe I'm just disappointed. I don't know. I somehow wanted more insight into her thinking at the beginning, but this is where she was and how she started her journey.

If I'm being honest with myself, mom's medication habit and how she communicates it in the privacy of her diary scare me. I don't know what to expect, nor even what I hope to discover. Does she ever internalize how pain meds began to control her?

### Sunday, August 23, 1992

*"Mom's good friend Ruth gave this book to me. She said I should write down my thoughts each day and later would see how much I had improved. Ruth is a very sweet and wise lady, and right now, I need all the help I can get. So, I will start my diary today, and we'll see how it goes.*

*Well, it's been about one-and-a-half weeks since my surgery. My body looks horrible. I am trying very hard to fix my hair and my makeup. Everybody says it doesn't matter that I have lost my breast, but it matters to me. Actually, I think emotionally, I am doing fine. Most of the time, I am really upbeat, but I do have my moments. I'm worried about my mom and hubby. They take such good care of me, but I would rather be taking care of them. Ray is having to work very hard at*

*work because of the new store, and right now, he*
*is cutting the grass, and he is not physically able*
*to do that. Mom is downstairs cooking, and she*
*washes and cleans the house. I just wish I could do*
*those things for them. I guess helpless is the way*
*I feel, and I don't like that. Sometimes I think*
*everyone involved would be better off if I just*
*died. Sometimes I just get very tired fighting the*
*battle of life.*

Before the diagnosis, the summer of 1992 was a good time for mom and dad. Both of their boys had graduated from the University of Tennessee, got married, and had their first children. Tiffiny and I were blessed to welcome Ashley into our lives in the spring of 1991, and Rick, my younger brother, and his wife Rebecca had their only child, Brittany. Mom was so excited to be a grandparent and quickly became nana. She threw herself into connecting with Ashley. There wasn't anything that could keep her from her first grandchild. It was also special that it was a little girl. After raising two boys in a household overflowing with testosterone, a sweet little girl seemed only fair.

Dad was enjoying his job as a wholesale furniture salesman. He was good at it and confident in himself, his colleagues trusted him, and his clients wanted to do business with him. It was the highlight of his working career.

Mom finally found a job she loved. She worked at Martin Marietta in an administrative position, and her colleagues loved her. A pleaser at heart, she always went the extra mile to be helpful, get things done, and generally make her environment a better place to be. I remember her coworkers complimenting her in glowing terms. The praise would've seemed overstated had I not lived with her and knew she spent every waking moment of her life trying to dote on everyone in her realm. Her legacy at work survived. Three years ago, a former colleague of mom's pulled me aside and asked whether he could share something about my mom with me. Not knowing what was coming next, I apprehensively said yes. With a tear in his eye, he said, "Your mom was the best. She brought a smile to everyone's face. There wasn't anything about her caring soul that was fake. She was genuine to the core. The office was never the same after she left. She was and is terribly missed."

Hearing these words made me proud, but it also provided a sad reminder that mom was never self-confident enough to acknowledge her impact. Aware she was making people happy? Yes. Able to translate that into a greater feeling of self-worth? Sadly, I don't think so. Nevertheless, her work finally was adding to her happiness.

In the first weeks of August 1992, a peaceful, carefree, comfortable life was shattered during an intimate moment when dad felt a large lump in mom's breast. Roughly the size of a grape, the lump seemingly came out of nowhere. Mom had received a routine mammography less than a year earlier. It was incomprehensible that it was cancer. So, what was it?

Mom didn't share her concern or the sudden scheduled

test with her family until the results were known. It was breast cancer, and surgery was scheduled immediately.

Mom and I talked almost every day, so when I saw her number on my cell phone, I was happy to answer. Without delay, mom said, "Mike, I have breast cancer, and I need you to come home." I was 25 years old; mom was 46.

Our family didn't have a history of cancer. I couldn't even think of any distant relatives who ever had it. I didn't know how to process what I was being told, or what was happening, and I damn sure didn't have a clue what was coming. Until you've been through it or witnessed someone close to you suffer from the disease and the brutal treatments, you can't appreciate the damage that's about to occur—damage to the patient's body, mind, soul, and relationships. It's complete destruction.

On that sunny, hot August afternoon, I wasn't thinking about any of the misery that was coming, I just needed to get to mom, and fast. Without delay, I journeyed home and quickly gave mom a hug. If I'm being honest, I felt uncomfortable hugging her. I don't know why, I just did. This was uncharted territory: Mom always had been the loving caregiver, and now it was my turn.

My unease grew. Mom told me the doctors had prepared her for the possibility that they may need to remove more than just the lump—possibly the whole breast. She said, "I'm scared." I remained silent. What could I say? She continued: "Mike, I need you to be there when I wake up. I want you to be the one to tell me what they did. Can you do that for me?" "Of course, I can," I mumbled, but I wasn't sure what I'd agreed to. Obviously, I'd speak with the doctor, understand what he said, and be in the room when she awakens——but why didn't she want dad in the room and just me?

The next morning, mom had surgery. It took a long time. I don't remember how long, but it seemed like forever. Eventually, the doctor came out and spoke with dad and me. Dad immediately left the waiting room. He didn't leave the hospital, but I don't know where he went. I was steered to the hospital room to wait for mom. I sat in the dark and cried because I was scared for mom, I cried because I was afraid I'd let her down, I cried because I was pissed. I just cried.

An hour or so passed, then they wheeled mom into the room. She was asleep. A long stretch of time passed before she opened her eyes. With tears welling up, she asked, "What happened?" "They took your breast, mom." I replied. "OK," she said as she closed her eyes, tears trickling down her cheeks.

That was over 30 years ago, and I still don't know how to process the experience. Why did she want me to be the one? I'll never know. I didn't ask her, and her diary doesn't offer any clues.

To be sure, as a man, I can't begin to understand what this means to a woman. I didn't then, and I don't today. Unable to process how this would impact her, I did the only thing I could do: I promised myself I'd do everything I could to protect her——whatever that meant.

As I read her initial diary entries, it isn't hard for me to believe her reaction and the words she wrote about her body. She felt disfigured. The surgery had claimed a private part of her body, and she didn't like how she looked. I'm sure this is a common feeling women have when they're forced into this procedure. I'm also sure that well-intentioned words from loved ones don't make it better, but what else can we say?

Her diary entry about her body didn't surprise me, but her words questioning whether we'd be better off if she were dead were devastating. Mom was a pleaser and a caregiver. On some level, she needed to take care of people to be happy. This elicits the questions: No matter what happened or what we did, could she ever have felt comfortable being the recipient of care? At this point in her life, she needed to be cared for, but it obviously pained her. On one hand, her family needed to step up and take care of her. On the other hand, she hated to be cared for. To make matters worse, her immediate family didn't have experience in this role. We were lost.

Fortunately for mom, her mom, Estelle, lived in an apartment connected to mom and dad's house. The consummate caregiver, and the one who taught mom the art of worrying about someone, lived under the same roof. It was a blessing, but it introduced a dynamic that mom already started referencing just days after her surgery: the need to be helped, and the need to be the helper—an emotional conflict showing itself in the earliest of days, foreshadowing challenges to come.

### Monday, August 24, 1992

*Today is a good day; the sun is shining. Mom and*

*I had a good talk over coffee this morning. Grace and Mr. and Mrs. Ramsey came to visit today. I am trying to write all the thank-you notes, and it is really taking a long time, but that is because people were so kind to me during this horrible ordeal. Brenda Matula called today, and I talked to both boys. Ray is still very tired, but his spirits are better and so are mine. Tomorrow, a trip to the hospital for a sonogram. I am nervous about that.*

Mom graduated from West High School in the spring of 1964. Scholarship in hand, she was headed to Sewanee to study math. Sewanee, known as the University of the South, is a small liberal arts school founded in 1857 by the Episcopal Church in the town of Sewanee, Tennessee. The campus sits on a 13,000-acre landscape that boasts beautiful scenery atop the Cumberland Plateau. Voted in 2011 as one of the most scenic college campuses in the country, Sewanee has a unique combination of beautiful topography with stunning gothic architecture. Jokingly called Tennessee's Hogwarts, the campus' serene setting would've been a perfect place for mom to have studied. A quiet, off-the-beaten-path town, hidden from the wild 1960s college scene, Sewanee offered the perfect transition from a protected blue-collar upbringing to a world of higher education.

Having raised the first member of the family with an opportunity to earn a college degree, Tommy and Estelle had accomplished a task that seemed daunting, if not impossible. They provided their offspring with a chance to have a better life. However, fate was about to intervene.

Mom was a popular teenager whom her classmates and sisters admired. Despite having shouldered responsibility for helping her working parents raise two younger sisters, she excelled in school and lived a respectable life that made her parents proud. There were occasional boyfriends, but it was the early '60s in a small conservative town that felt more like the '50s than the free-spirited, rebellious decade that followed. Mom once told me, "Looking back, I was naïve and sheltered. I was raised in a strict Southern Baptist household, and I lived within the expectations of what that meant."

On a hot, mid-June night, mom and her youngest sister Pam went to watch the Knoxville Smokies, a Southern League AA minor league baseball team play a game at the now-defunct Bill Meyer Stadium. The 6,400-seat stadium was nestled east of downtown amid turn-of-the-century manufacturing buildings, most notably the Standard Knitting Mill towering above the left-field fence. Just beginning its second decade hosting the team, the stadium and its environs were just what you would've expected––Americana at its best. It was at this game that she met dad. Sitting in the row behind mom and Pam, dad struck up a conversation and playfully teased Pam to get mom's attention. It worked.

Dad had a tough childhood. His parents, Cecil and Betty, had a tragically similar story to mom's parents, but they hadn't done as well. With little education, and the products of two struggling families, they scraped to get by. In fact, at different times, dad was forced to live with Betty's mom, Furn Burnett, because his parents couldn't, or wouldn't, care for his needs. Dad's time with his grandmother was spent in a tiny house in Vestal, a south Knoxville neighborhood known for its tough residents and tough times. Dad's grandmother was a chiseled woman whose life spanned most of the 20th century. She had eight children, seven of which lived long enough to raise their own families. I remember her hugging me. She was made of grit, bone, and roughness. She had to be. To be the caregiver for a young man in a community where bad things could happen was a full-time job. She loved dad, and he loved her. When dad talked of his childhood, he talked of her and how she raised him.

Despite his unsettled childhood, dad finished high school, graduating in 1962 from Ringgold High School in Ringgold, Georgia, after having only attended the school for his senior year. Going to college never crossed dad's mind. His opportunity lied in the Army, and he enlisted immediately after high school. He was on leave the night he went to watch the Smokies play.

It must've been a whale of a night at the old ballgame because mom and dad immediately began dating and were inseparable for the three weeks before dad was shipped off to Germany and his next deployment. Their tearful goodbye was full of promises they both believed would be kept. And they were. Dad wrote mom every day. By the third week, dad was professing his love, and in a fateful, emotional letter, asked mom to marry him. It's hard for me to imagine a time when this was normal, but it was all too common. Mom and dad both admitted they didn't know anything about each other, and without the benefit of today's technology, they only had daily letters to fill in the blanks.

When dad asked mom to marry him, nothing was discussed explicitly about her plans to go to college. It was just understood that if she married dad, he expected her to forgo college and join him. I can only speculate, but it isn't hard for me to believe he asked her so quickly, knowing that if she had left in the fall of 1964 for Sewanee, they likely would never have become a couple. I don't blame dad. He wasn't being nefarious. He was in love and, like mom, followed the roadmap he understood. You get married, build a life, and get on with it.

I don't know whether mom recognized her decision's significance. Whether it was a conscious or unconscious process, mom had to choose between college and life with a man she fell in love with over a few dates and a couple dozen letters. In a very real sense, she was following the path her mother had taken. Without college as an option, Estelle found her man and tied her hopes and dreams to a relative stranger hoping they would find a better life.

Mom did the same. She picked romance and a man over her personal dreams. I grew up unaware that mom chose dad over college; however, I always was keenly aware that mom harbored an innate feeling that she hadn't pursued things the way she wanted.

Twenty-five years later, it was obvious to me that a void was still there that never left her. I could feel it when we talked about her dreams and her life, but that no longer mattered. She'd built her life with dad, they were happy, and they loved each other. And now, they were embarking on a fight for her life.

### Tuesday, August 25, 1992

*Today will be a two-part message. At 11 a.m. today, I am going for a sonogram to look at a cyst on my left kidney. Everyone says it is a water cyst (probably) and I should not worry, but I am worried. I'm scared to death. We'll see how the rest of the day goes.*

*Good news—the doctor's office called and said not to worry—the cyst on my kidney was a water cyst. No connection to the cancer. But I am very tired, and for some reason, depressed. Maybe I am just tired.*

I was once told that a cancer diagnosis is like a visit to an amusement park's signature roller coaster. The first time you ride it, each turn and drop are new and, thus, filled with uncertainty. The initial experience creates a fear borne of not knowing what's coming next, and an innate anxiety caused by the expectation of pending twists and turns. Strangely, each subsequent time you ride the same coaster, you know what's coming, so the surprise is gone, but the emotion isn't. Whether it's the anticipation of what you know is coming, or the thrill of restrained terror, for most, a roller coaster still elicits a reaction no matter how many times you ride it.

Cancer treatment is its own version of a wild ride. For a

new patient, each new step of your cancer journey creates uncertainty, fear, drama, dread, and, oddly enough, even hopeful anticipation. Every test, doctor's visit, phone call, article you read, and treatment you receive is packed with emotion. For mom, this was all new. She had no history to rely on or roadmap to know what was next. Even for the most confident person, entering this volatile vortex is debilitating.

Mom was a strong woman. There was always a smile, and she was equally quick at channeling her inner toughness and, if necessary, putting those who crossed her in their place. Her toughness was more than skin deep. She was raised to be tough. The early, and pitiful, death of her dad during Thanksgiving week in 1976 at the age of 59 and her own health scare in her early 40s had shown her that life could be harsh. At home, her marriage wasn't volatile, but dad was a challenge. In the role of an old-school wife, mom was willing to endure dad's emotions and the disappointment she felt from not being the total woman she wanted to be. Dad wasn't abusive, nor did he drink, but he was demanding and at times unfair.

Witnessing this as a child, I held mom and her strength in the highest regard. It never occurred to me that she could be vulnerable or fall victim to a feeling of helplessness, but I was wrong. A few short weeks into her cancer treatments, mom was expressing, privately in her diary, a sense of hopelessness and fear that surprises me.

Looking back, I don't recall knowing mom already was in this place. Was this a failure on my part and those around her? Did she not feel like she could share her feelings with us? Or maybe we weren't receptive to her fears. Maybe seeing her as always being strong was unfair and misstated her realities. I don't know.

What I do believe is that cancer changes everything. It strips down whatever walls existed and exposes any and all hidden truths or secrets. All bets are off. I wish I'd known that at the time. I wish I'd dropped my biases and allowed myself to enter her new world, open to helping any way I could. I didn't do that. Maybe it's because I couldn't or maybe didn't know what I was doing, nor what was coming next.

The news that the cyst wasn't related to cancer obviously was welcomed. This was our first little affirmation that the cancer hadn't metastasized. Like all other reports, mom shared the news with all of us. What I don't recall her sharing was that she was feeling down or depressed. She kept that to herself.

Clearly, mom already was struggling with more than just cancer. There were darker demons present and growing. Mom unwillingly had strapped herself into the roller coaster, and each curve or drop was about to surprise her and create unwanted emotions.

# CHAPTER 3

### August 27, 1992

*Returned to Dr. Vickers' Office. Removed rest of staples, but left tube in. Tube was very, very painful. He prescribed me 10 Lorcet.*

### Saturday, August 29, 1992

*I haven't written for the last few days, and there is no particular reason. My emotions have been all over the place. One moment I feel good, and my spirits are great, and the next, I am ready to cry. On Wednesday, I went to Dr. Vickers. They removed half of my staples, but left the drainage tube in. They said if they took it out, I would probably have to have the fluid drain off with a needle. I have had several visitors the latter part of the week and lots of cards and calls. People have been really good to me. I've talked with Dee about the chemo and Frances about a bra and prostheses. Today is beautiful outside, cool and sunny. I was letting myself really get down, then I asked Ray to take me for a ride. We put the top down on the convertible and rode down by the river and onto Kingston Pike. The sunshine and fresh air really helped. I guess I am doing pretty good, but I still feel awfully depressed. I know my prognosis is good, but I just can't get excited about anything. Ashley and Tiffiny are coming tomorrow, and I'm not even excited about that. Will I ever be the same?*

I N A VERY REAL SENSE, learning to live with cancer is about learning to enjoy the passage of time. As humans, we're at our best when we have something to do and a desire to do it. For mom, she was about her family, her friends, and her work. She leaned into most days.

However, her diagnosis altered her schedule and, obviously, her perspective. She was now resigned to measuring her day, her time spent, her happiness, with the knowledge that there was something in her body trying to kill her.

We all have heard older people lament how time seems to move so fast. "Seems like only yesterday...." I heard my uncle once say that about an event that happened 20 years prior. When I was young, this mindset made little sense to me. Every day is the same amount of time for all of us. The number of hours in a day doesn't change as we get older; our perception of time changes.

When you're five, a year is mathematically a long time. After all, it's roughly 20% of your lifetime. However, when you're 60, a year represents 1.6% of your life. Older people have more experience, and these experiences start to blend together. Studies have shown that for older people, the more diverse their day, the more likely they are to experience time in a "normal sense." If they look back on their week, and it was filled with various activities that aren't repeated, it's more likely they'll view their week within the context of seven distinct days. If every day is exactly the same, a week isn't a summation of seven days, but rather one long day without distinction, and strangely, it feels like it flew by.

However, it's also true that routine and a predictable schedule also have been shown to lead to happiness and even a longer life. When individuals find their place in the world and pleasure in their repeatable activities, there's a comfort that develops, and even peacefulness. Life might be moving "fast," but for most people, they're content with a life without much change.

Now imagine for a moment that you find yourself in a situation in which you're stuck in a routine that doesn't bring happiness. Time seems to be slipping away at a rapid pace, and the routine you find yourself in isn't bringing peace, but rather a constant reminder of something dreadful.

All these years removed from mom's fight to live, I've wondered how I'd react if I was in the same situation. What would I do? We've all heard about people who, faced with a terrible diagnosis, rally and begin to live their best lives. They tackle each day trying to do something that day to mark the day as different. How are they able to do that? I'm sure they have bad days, but we don't hear about those days. In any event, it's remarkable to witness a person embracing life while living a tragedy.

I can't even begin to know how I'd react. Privately, I always hoped I'd live differently than mom. I've harbored a silent disappointment that mom settled on a path that was submissive to her disease. My critical judgment of mom's attitude toward her diagnosis bothered me for years. What a jerk I am to judge her. She's the one who had the disease.

In hindsight, my conclusions about mom were wrong. Mom wasn't built to react differently than she did. She always adapted to whatever life gave her and did the best she could. When she was given this challenge, it became her focus. It hung over her and defined her day, every day. Her routine became simple. If there was diversity in her days, it revolved around the cancer—a doctor's appointment, test results, prescriptions filled, and constant pain.

The things that brought her joy before the cancer didn't provide joy now. A visit from her first granddaughter would've been her happiest event of the week before she became sick. Now she expressed indifference. Mom was, and already had fallen, into a cycle of basic existence; therefore, her happiness was tied to the routine of living with cancer.

This elicits the question: What could we have done? Honestly, I don't know. The family thought we were giving her the support she needed. I know we thought we were, but it appears we weren't. Reflecting on this time and our response leaves me cold.

Mom's entry is more direct about her feelings than I recall her expressing to us, which tells me we weren't listening, i.e., actively engaged in understanding where she was and what she needed. I didn't feel like we weren't helpful, but we were living our lives and were very ill-prepared to support her.

A diary is a private, safe place to share personal feelings and release your burdens. Mom was expressing her thoughts to herself. What if she'd shared them with us? What if we'd been more receptive? What if we knew what the hell we were doing? I don't pretend to believe it would've changed the outcome, but it might have altered her journey.

### September 1, 1992

*Returned to Vickers. Still left tube in. Gave me 15 Lorcet for pain and reflux. He was afraid I was going to get an infection. I was absolutely miserable at this time.*

### Friday, September 4, 1992

*This has been a good week. Tiffiny and Ashley came up Sunday to spend the week. I was afraid that this would not work out as well, but it did. Mom came through as always. She was always there to help with food or whatever was needed. I was able to enjoy Ashley. I couldn't pick her up, but I could still enjoy her just playing on the floor. Of course, I made many trips to the doctors. I saw Dr. Vickers twice, Dr. Kerns and Dr. Barnett. This week is going to be a big one. Tuesday, I will finally get my tube out of my side. On Thursday, I will go to day surgery and have a shunt put in my chest to receive chemo, and Friday, I get to start the big chemo. Ray has been great through this. He went to Dr. Kerns with me. I am afraid of the chemo, but yet I am anxious to get started so I can see what is going to happen. I guess that I will always live with the fear of the Big C coming back. Sometimes I feel pretty good about the future, and sometimes, I just get tired and think what is the use? Well, I guess it will just be day to day. Right now, that's all I can do, and for the next four days, I have nothing to worry about.*

Doug Holladay, founder of PathNorth and author of *Rethinking Success*, quotes Peter Buffett when he writes, "We're all born into someone else's story." It's true. We don't choose our life circumstances or our parents. We have no control over how our parents live, how they raise us, nor the opportunities we have. We're dependent on those who brought us into the world to protect, provide, and teach us the ways of the world so that someday we can, if not thrive, at least exist independently. Obviously, DNA determines much of who we are and what we become, but our life experiences define us.

From my perspective, the similarities between mom

and her mom—"mamaw" to us grandkids—were clear to me growing up. Time has only confirmed my view that those two shared a life story that was some parts DNA and a heavy dose of life. They prioritized family and offered unconditional love. They were kind and tough. Mom once hit me on the head with a broomstick because I arrived home well past curfew. She quickly followed with a sweet hug, told me she loved me, and kissed me goodnight. They also would defend their loved ones—aggressively if necessary.

In 1986, I was a walk-on football player for the University of Tennessee. We played Auburn at Auburn. After the game, my mom, dad, and mamaw wanted to be outside the locker room to greet me before I got on the team bus. Unfortunately, to do that, they had to pass through the Auburn student section while wearing paraphernalia that showcased they had a family member from the opposing team. As you might imagine, they received a fair amount of verbal abuse. Dad claimed he was more than prepared to hear whatever, put his head down, and get through the barrage. However, mom and mamaw had other ideas. As they later told it, "We weren't interested in the abusive comments from frat boys from Auburn." They chose to respond with aggression. They didn't get violent, just intense, and as I understand it, it didn't take long for the throng of students to realize that they needed to get out of the way and leave these wild Tennessee girls alone.

I always find this story funny because they wouldn't hurt a fly—unless the fly was hurting someone they loved.

They had a deeply embedded need to protect. Sometimes it manifested itself in funny, memorable stories. Other times the need to protect became the defining current driving the tone and tenor of everyday life.

Mamaw was born into an impoverished family with 10 siblings. She was taught how to work, fight, and protect. Years later, she became the breadwinner, caretaker, and rock of the family. She was forced into it, and if she was discouraged by her lot, she didn't express it. I used to laugh at how mamaw worried about things. Years later, it makes sense. When you've lived in hard times, you're always aware something could be lurking around the corner to cause trouble. Mamaw's habit of worrying wasn't a personality quirk; it was a lifetime of experience telling her that bad stuff happens. Mom continued the tradition. She was a worrier. Again, DNA was at work, but so was life.

As the oldest child of Tommy and Estelle, mom had to grow up fast. There was no way to shield her from her family's struggles. She often talked about the moment she realized she was poor. It was a blisteringly cold day in November 1956. Mom was 10, and the family was living on Detroit Avenue on the Tennessee campus. It was a football Saturday, and her house was less than a quarter of a mile from the stadium. Behind their house were train tracks that brought game day fans to Neyland Stadium. As the train pulled to a stop behind her house, fans departed the train full of laughter and enthusiasm, but what stood out most to mom was what they were wearing. "The men wore these dapper wool coats, and the women had beautiful mink coats. They were dressed like movie stars. I barely had a coat to keep me warm." On the surface, it seems like a meaningless memory, but it stuck with mom forever.

As an adult, her chance to become a caregiver presented itself almost immediately. I was born with a cleft lip and palate, a birth defect presenting itself as a disfigured upper lip and opening in the roof of the mouth. Mom never shared with me how she received the news. In fact, even as an adult, I don't recall her ever talking much about that time. What I know about that period in my life I gleaned from others who were around.

Mom was very protective of me. She didn't want people to make fun of me or how I looked and sought out the best surgeon she could find to repair the defect. He did a wonderful job. Today, my childhood birth defect isn't detectable, but mom's efforts to correct the defect weren't what stood out. She invested energy into my development and growth, and was unwavering in ensuring that I was taken care of. This included significant work to correct a speech impediment that resulted from the cleft lip and palate. In fact, I really struggled to speak as a child. There were years of therapy sessions coupled with mom dutifully practicing with me. In time, the speech challenges faded, but not before the fateful moment when I was five and visiting the surgeon who repaired my lip. A few years removed from the procedure, he wanted to see how I looked and was progressing.

Mom loved telling this story. It captured her pride, but also her love of laughter. As mom told it, at the end of the doctor's visit, the surgeon wanted to hear how my speech was doing. To encourage me to speak, he sat me on the window ledge and asked me to tell him what I saw outside the window. At this moment, mom felt panic. Despite the progress I'd made with my speech, there remained one nagging, recurring problem: I always replaced the letters TR with F, so any word that was supposed to be pronounced with those letters was altered. Reminded of this, mom always smiled when retelling the story and thanked God a truck didn't pass by the window.

Everyone should have someone in their life who loves them unconditionally and is willing to give so much of themselves. Mom blessed me with her love, protection, spirit to push forward, positivity, and strength. Everything I've become was influenced in those early days when I faced a future that could've held challenges and a lifetime of insecurity. Reflecting on those formative days and how mom was in my corner, I'm humbled.

Mom's need to care for others was in her soul. She knew how to give, but didn't know how to be the recipient. Life hadn't prepared her to be taken care of, and now she was facing a time when she was dependent on others. Simultaneously, mamaw was in the house, and even though she desperately didn't want mom to be sick and to need her, she was more than experienced and capable of offering the kind of care she'd spent a lifetime providing. On the surface, this was good news, and all these years later, I still think it was a blessing. However, it also created a strange––and I'd argue––unhealthy environment.

Because of so many shared life experiences and circumstances, they tended to process things the same way. In the early days, the closeness and daily support looked comfortable, but I can't ignore what was developing. Obviously, in the initial weeks, mom was grateful for Mamaw's presence. I may learn as I continue reading the diary that she never reached a point where she expresses anything that contradicts her current feelings, but for me, I saw an almost circular loop of thinking and mindset.

Over the years, I've thought about how things might have been different. How would mom have reacted if mamaw hadn't been there? Prior to her illness, I viewed mom as a doer, someone who would grab a problem, own it, and in time kick its ass. After cancer, in my view, mom took on more of a victim mindset. I concluded, maybe unfairly, that this was because mamaw was there and, through no fault of her own, took care of mom like you would a child. I think that stripped mom of the need or desire to march onward with a different approach.

I admit that I could be completely wrong about this. Unless there's some breakthrough in the upcoming pages of her diary, I'll likely never truly know why mom reacted the way she did. I want to believe mom became more of a victim because of something inadvertently influencing her. That would make me feel better, but honestly, that's a self-absorbed need. Who knows how I would have, or will, act when faced with a threat to my existence? Truth be told, I hope the pages of mom's diary offer some guidance to influence my response to some future personal crisis.

*September 8, 1992*

*Returned to Vickers. Removed the tube. I thought I had died and gone to heaven. I had two of my best days after that. I prepaid for the prosthesis. Went to lunch, shopped a little, and went to my nephew's football game.*

I find joy in these few simple sentences. It's the first time I'm reading an entry that sounds like mom. I know I'm reaching, but until now, mom's reflections have seemed desperate, wanting, and void of optimism. The simple act of removing a physical reminder that you're sick, combined with a forward-looking purchase and some pleasant activities, brought joy and resulted in a positively toned entry.

I know it's not that simple, and yet it elicits a question that has lingered with me for years: How do those close to the afflicted person act? Do we carry on and exist as though life is normal and avoid frequent acknowledgment of the disease, or do we continuously ask them how they're doing?

It's common for all of us, when chatting with family or friends, to begin a conversation with "How are you doing?" It's often how we greet each other. Usually when we say this, we don't really want anything more than a superficial response. It's an inquiry to show we care that's usually followed by an equally quick "I'm good," "I'm great," or "I'm shitty." The response generally reflects the personality of the person asked, and that's that. We then all move on.

But when you ask someone who's dangerously sick, the benign question makes a deeper impact. I always struggled with this. Prior to the fall of 1992, when I spoke with mom, I consistently sought to bring our families' historical optimism to our calls. "Hey mom, how are you?" I'd ask. This would be followed by some energetic, positive response. That was how we communicated. It brought comfort to me and served as private reinforcement from the person who had built my foundation.

But the moment she got sick, that all changed. Cancer framed her view of the world and provided a prism for how she saw and heard everything. Forevermore, when I asked her how she was doing, she interpreted it as a question about her illness. On some level, that's what I was asking, but on another, I was trying subconsciously to steer her back to pre-cancer mom. Writing this, I understand my goal's absurdity. It sounds like I was being selfish, and I was. You can't get do-overs in life. I wanted to go back. No cancer, no threat to life, no pain.

I also wanted to be a light for the future. It's this point I can't reconcile. What's the balance between being there in the moment and trying to experience the suffering with the person you love, and bringing optimism and an alternative perspective of hope and normalcy? How can you show empathy without spending all your energy focusing on the misery of reality?

I don't know. Presumably there's a way to demonstrate both empathy and normalcy, but that seems ambitious. We're all imperfect, vulnerable, emotional beings who cannot live near perfection, let alone communicate perfectly in any given environment. Combine that obvious truth with the other person's emotion, and it's no wonder that conversations with sick loved ones miss the mark. Frankly, I wanted mom to be mom. I wanted to feel lifted when we spoke, and my playbook was the same as it always had been. I led with a simple inquiry seeking to elicit a comforting response from the person who was always there for me.

Looking back, I fear that I failed miserably. My transition from receiver of emotional support to giver was lacking. I didn't understand what was happening, and mom was effective at hiding her feelings. She continued her role as caretaker, but privately, she needed us. We still yearned for her comfort and maternal love, and she was afraid she was dying.

At some point in her journey, my awareness of what I was failing to do kicked in, but it was too late. She needed us from the beginning—when she was scared, when she was developing her sense of what the future would bring, when she was establishing the norms for how she would live with cancer. I don't know when I became better at balancing empathy with normalcy. I just know that by the time I started the balancing act, her new normal was very distorted from what it was before. It may be silly to try to reconstruct this now. I just wish I had context back then and was able to consider my role from day one.

Two decades later, this simple entry brings a smile to my face. It harkens to a time when mom was shining bright, and I was bathed in that optimism. I feel blessed to revisit this because I so desperately want my memories of this period to include signs of happiness. I trust that this modest passage will live with me for a while. Unfortunately for mom, her happiness was temporary.

### September 10, 1992

*Went into day surgery to have a port-o-cath put in. The surgery was not fun, but survivable. Dr. Vickers gave me a prescription for Percocet. I think he gave me 15. The pain was so great that night that I took 10 of the Percocet from the time I left day surgery until the next day.*

### September 12, 1992

*Chemo shots started. Dr. Kerns' associate agreed to give me more Percocet for the first few days. The first day, I slept. The second day, I started the shots, which caused muscle aches and pains. I had a few Percocets left for the first few days, then the torment began. I called Dr. Kerns' office, and they said yes, it was supposed to hurt. I said I thought it was supposed to be for three days. They said it was different with different folks and that the Neupogen shots would make it worse.*

Billions of charitable dollars and private sector clinical research have altered how women with breast cancer are treated. Today, oncologists attack cancer by first identifying the genetic mutations in the discovered breast cancer cells. This allows the physician to prepare a treatment regimen prior to performing any invasive procedure.

Once a plan is determined, there's a clear commitment to preserve, if possible, the breast and extract the cancer with a targeted, contained procedure called a lumpectomy. These approaches, combined with drugs designed to target various mutations, have resulted in marked improvements in patients' quality of life and pre-metastatic cancer survival rates. That's obviously good news, but when I compare today's treatment protocols to what mom experienced from the time of her initial diagnosis to the launch of her first days of clinical interventions, I'm profoundly sad. I feel no ill will toward the doctors and what they offered her, and I think they did the best they could. I have to believe that. Nevertheless, it's obvious, 30 years later, that she faced her battle with the odds stacked against her.

Treatment for breast cancer in the early 1990s was blunt, aggressive, nonspecific, and unfortunately only marginally effective. Immediately following a breast cancer diagnosis, a mastectomy was performed, and chemotherapy was scheduled. It was accepted dogma that the primary task was to stop and kill cancer cells before they grow and spread. Chemotherapy was believed to be the best option to destroy cancer cells, but unfortunately, its effects were indiscriminate. In war, they call this collateral damage. In 1992, the resulting destruction to a human body from chemo was called treatment.

As is often the case with historical medical treatments, assessing them in the light of today's knowledge can make them seem barbaric. I'm not sure mom's treatment would fit the category of barbarism, but it damn sure was brutal.

Mom welcomed August 1992 having no discernable symptoms, believing she was in good health and living her normal life. She didn't know she had a disease that, left undetected or untreated, certainly would kill her. As best as she could tell, life was grand. Thirty days later, her life was in danger.

Mom was scared, and I can feel it in her writing. Why wouldn't she be? Chemo was then, and is still now, feared and dreaded. A simple inquiry today on Google about chemo brings up countless studies and articles about its side effects, lasting impact, known negatives, and even stark questions asking, "Is chemo worth it?" Thirty years ago, chemo had a very dark reputation. All a patient knew about chemo prior to their first treatment was what family, friends, nurses, and doctors told them—and it wasn't pretty. Horror stories filled with anecdotes and examples told of unimaginable misery. As humans, we typically can process fear from what we know will happen, but it's much harder to prepare for fear of the unknown.

It was difficult for mom to accept that for her to get better, she must punish her body. This isn't like having a torn meniscus and undergoing surgery to repair it. Post-op hurts, but you know why you did it; you were in pain before the operation. In mom's case, she didn't know she was sick and had no symptoms.

In all the years I've reflected on this, I'm ashamed to admit I've never really allowed myself to feel empathy and understanding for this moment in mom's life. She seemed alone, unsure, wanting to trust, but doubtful.

I'm not suggesting that mom should've avoided the

best available treatments or alternatives recognized by the medical community as best practices. She lived in a time when this is what was available to her, and I'm glad she chose to fight.

However, this moment in mom's journey marked a transition. She would never be the same. During her remaining days, she had good times and periods when she felt OK, but in hindsight, her treatment, led by the chemo regimen and all the supporting medication, damaged her. As she reclined on a plastic-covered medical chair with an IV in her arm, it was delivering a form of poison.

And where were we? Afraid, unsure, silent, and wholly unprepared to support mom during her trials. I was aware at the time that I wasn't getting it right. I knew I needed to do more, but I didn't know what that meant. I still don't. I promised myself I'd protect her. I don't know whether I was doing that.

### September 16, 1992

*I went back to Dr. Vickers to get staples removed from my port-of-cath. While I was in the building, I went upstairs to Dr. Kerns' office and told them something had to be done. They did a blood check and said my white blood count was 3.2 and my red was OK. I said, "Can't you please give me something for the aching?" They said try Tylenol. By Thursday, I was sick. I called Dr. Kerns' office back, and they said they would return my call. While waiting impatiently, I called a pharmacy friend of mine. I told him what I was taking and asked if*

*Soma would hurt me since it was for muscle aches and pain. He said it would not hurt, but it would intensify the effects. At that point, I didn't care. So, I took one. It was wonderful. It helped my pain. In the meantime, Dr. Kerns' office called and said they were calling me in Loracet Extra Strength. I took them for a long time, and they helped some.*

*On Wednesday night, the pain was so great, Ray called Mike and said I was depressed. He was scared, etc. Mike called my sister or sisters and together they decided I needed help. The only thing I'm upset about is why didn't they talk to me? I would have gone to see Dr. Barnett. I have one son 300 miles away, a sister 200 miles away, another sister 20 miles away, and a husband I see about three hours a day, and they decided I needed help. Why didn't they ask mom? She is with me all the time. For someone with a breast removed, day surgery just a week before, and chemo all in one month, I thought I was doing good. The chemo was unbearable, and I'm saying I may not take it anymore. If that makes me crazy, then I am crazy. I have one thing to be thankful for—no nausea.*

Mom wasn't crazy, but she was a mess. Four days into her first round of chemo, and she's chasing pain medication. The strategy was easy to execute. If you were being treated by a disconnected group of doctors, and they weren't actively communicating, you could seek, and likely receive, multiple prescriptions for pain relief.

This is a little harder to do today. Technology has created better transparency, i.e., better information combined with a medical community that's wiser to the problems of prescription drug addictions has given doctors greater ability to identify patients who are angling for pain meds.

In the fall of 1992, mom wasn't having difficulty getting her hands on pain pills. She was actively and aggressively seeking pain relief from her surgeon, oncologist, pharmacist, and internist, and they were obliging.

I believe in personal accountability, and ultimately, this was on mom, but the doctors were complicit in this. I don't know whether they thought they were helping or just pacifying her so they didn't have to listen to her complain. I understand that she was relentless. Even in the early days, this became her driving focus; however, I felt then and do now that the doctors straddled the line of empathy and compassion for her pain, annoyance with her whining, and a desire to give her what she wanted so she would leave them alone. Regardless of their motivation, mom's doctors were unhelpful and contributed to her dependence.

Looking back, we lost this war during the first battle. At the time, I didn't appreciate the depth of the problem. Until this moment, mom never demonstrated, at least to me, an addictive personality. She didn't drink or smoke. There were few signs signaling what was ahead or alarms giving us a warning of this spiraling problem. I was in the dark, and acted like it.

I remember dad reaching out to me. I remember calling mom's internist, Dr. Barnett, who was a wonderful man who cared for mom. He warned me of what was to come, and I don't know why I didn't hear him. I suppose I processed what was said to me just like most things I was told: in one ear and out the other. It's amazing how smart you think you are when you're in your 20s. Always certain, occasionally right.

Calling Dr. Barnett helped some. He spoke with the other physicians, and at a minimum, alerted them to mom's tendency to seek pills for pain. But it was like spraying water from a garden hose on a forest fire. Maybe it'll put out a hot spot or two, but heavy winds, dry conditions, and uncontrolled flames rage on.

Although I know she was in pain, and I accept that she didn't have a high threshold to endure pain, this feels like more was going on than how bad it hurt. I don't understand. I really don't. I've tried to understand why she reacted this way. I have no doubt we made mistakes, but this feels like the root cause, and the management of it, was beyond our ability to handle as a family.

Her frustration that we didn't talk to her is fair. In a perfect world, no one should feel managed, especially by people who care for you. On some level, I wish I'd reached out to her directly, but today, I'm in my 50s and have the benefit of knowing what happens, and yet I still don't know what I would've said to her. I chose an easier path: I called her doctor. I don't recall during this episode ever speaking directly to her about it.

In a very real sense, this is the first example of a wall that was forming between us. A month removed from mom asking me to tell her what happened to her breast, and I can't find the words to talk to her about her growing habit. It's absurd, and I was weak, but I wasn't the only one adding bricks to the wall. Mom also was creating her own moat. She was keeping things from us, holding in her feelings, fears, hopes, and expectations. I sense that she was sharing things with dad, but she wasn't sharing with me.

Maybe that's OK. I was her son, not her advisor or counselor. However, when you build a wall, brick by brick, over a long period of time, it's hard to notice it blocking your view.

Prior to cancer, mom and I talked every day. Eventually, that frequency would change. We grew more distant, and I think I know why. I wonder whether mom noticed, and whether her perspective found its way into her diary.

# CHAPTER 4

*September 24, 1992*

*Well, I haven't written in quite a while, but I am going to catch up from the chemo day. It was horrible. The first three days were not so bad. I slept most of the time. Then the pain started. It was unbearable. I took my shots. Tried to be brave because I thought I should be able to stand this if anyone could. On Tuesday, 9/12, I went to Dr. Vickers and had my staples removed. While I was there, I went to Dr. Kerns' office and told them about the pain. The nurses checked my blood and suggested I take Tylenol (oh, please). By the next day, I couldn't take it anymore. I called Dr. Kerns' office—they said they would call back. In the meantime, I called Dr. Berano and asked him if I could take Soma. After telling him everything I was taking, he told me it would not hurt me, would probably help me, but would intensify its effects. I took one; it did help, but I was thick-tongued and staggering. I had told Ray I didn't think I could take this anymore, and I was not going to take chemo anymore. He got on the phone with Mike, and after a family discussion, Mike called Dr. Barnett on Friday night. He said to get me in on Monday. He fixed everything. I was given pain medication and referred to a counselor, and now this has been one of the best weeks ever. Mom and I have gone places. Target, Red Lobster, Ray's store, Walmart and I went to a party for Larry. I'm good for about three hours, then I need a nap. But I feel great. I have to take chemo again one week from tomorrow. I'm scared, but I'm going to do it. I'm going to take it easy, take care of myself, and keep a positive attitude. I have an appointment next week to be fitted for a prosthesis. I am anxious to be back into normal clothes. I'm also going to check on getting a wig, just in case. My family is wonderful. They care so much about me, and I am thankful for them. On Monday, Dr. Barnett told me to go home, call my family, and tell them thanks for caring.*

I KNEW THE PROCESS OF WRITING this book parallel to reading the diary might have odd twists and turns, and the above entry offers the first example. As mom retells the story of her first days of chemo, the reflections are consistent with her entry from the week before. What strikes me is how she ends her comments. The positive, strong woman that raised me leaps off the page.

Countless memories of moments when mom propped me up, hugged me, told me I could do it, or that those who were doubting or hurting me were to be ignored fill my head. As you get older, you don't remember everything. In fact, memories seem selective.

Why are certain memories strong and other meaningful events recalled only when triggered? I don't know. It's true, though, and it's exactly how I'd describe my memories of mom. Almost without exception, when I think of mom before she had cancer, I think of a rock who was my best friend and my biggest supporter. I recall someone who sought happiness and positivity in everything, a hopeful spirit who found ways to believe in people and the brightness of life.

Her hopefulness defined me. Because of her, I believed that anything was possible, people could be trusted, it was OK—and actually important—to be a pleaser, and life was a joyous journey. Two decades after mom's death, I don't feel the same. I've invested a lot of energy considering why my world view is different. Have I changed? Has the world changed? Have my experiences driven me to accept that the basic tenets that mom instilled in me were invalid? Or maybe what's missing is mom providing me with a strong roadmap instilling in me strength and confidence to see opportunities, people, and the world through an all-things-are-possible lens.

In the intervening years, I've experienced countless times when people have counseled me that I'd find more success if I dreamed less, learned to be more critical, recognized obstacles, didn't care what people thought, and focused more on my own outcome. I'm sure they're right and that embracing that mindset leads to more success. I just don't believe it leads to personal happiness.

In the past two decades, I've lost my way. I'm not who I used to be. I know it, and I don't like it, or me. What I don't know is how to recapture what she instilled inside of me. How do I take my life experiences and focus on doing good. This is scary for me. I've proven to myself that I'm not making progress on my own, and mom isn't here to help.

I'm not afraid to grind it out, work hard, and invest in myself. Mom's diary offers a chance to do that. One month into her written story, and I'm beginning to believe there will be no magic moment. I could be wrong, but I'm preparing myself and internalizing this reality: gaining from this will require effort. Mom didn't write her diary for me; she wrote it for herself. If I am to regain her influence and impact on me, I'll have to do it through interpretation. It's my sincere hope that I can do that.

### September 25, 1992

*What a night. I can't sleep. If I get six hours of sleep, I am lucky. But it does give me a lot of great time to write. I write letters, notes, etc., but I wish I could sleep more. I am feeling good, but I get tired, and I guess part of that is not sleeping. I hope today is beautiful. I want to go to a movie. I want to make hay while the sun is shining because next Friday is chemo again.*

### Sunday, September 27, 1992

*It is a rainy, dreary day today, but I hope to get to go to church. Yesterday was a fun day. Sue, Richard, and their daughter Missy came down to pick up some furniture. It was so good to talk to them. We really do need to get together more. Mom and I went out to eat then saw a movie. Tennessee won their ballgame, so everyone is happy. I feel good, but I feel like I'm on a countdown to "C" day. I just have to stop thinking about it.*

### Monday evening, September 28, 1992

*This has been an up and down day. Very early this morning, things didn't seem so bright. Maybe it was the weather (gloomy). Then mom and I started repotting all of my plants. They really looked pretty. Had a nice visit from Bea (she brought some bread). Mom and I did a little shopping. But in the back of my mind, all I can think of is chemo. Ray's grandmother called tonight, and I feel so very sorry for her. I'm really down. I feel like I am on chemo death row.*

### Wednesday, September 30, 1992, 4 a.m.

*Well, yesterday was a real good day. The sun was shining; the air was cool. Mother and I cleaned the house. We vacuumed and dusted and cleaned the kitchen and bath. It sure looked good. The big event of the day was buying my new prosthesis. I could not believe how it felt. It was like a real breast. The weight of it and the softness and the way it shifted. It was the first time in weeks I felt somewhat normal. I didn't like how everyone was looking at me, and I just felt better about myself. Barbara came by and brought me four puzzles. She is such a thoughtful person. I am still having problems thinking about my chemo, but I think it is normal. I'm preparing for it by doing things like writing out checks for bills, buying my medicine, and just doing anything I can that I think I might need to do next week. Maybe it won't be as bad this time.*

A few days of simple joy. It's nice to see. Mom sharing little things that made her feel good makes me feel good. I can see her soft smile as she greeted friends, her laughing during playful conversations, her peaceful face as she wrote to those she cared about. It reminds me that for mom, happiness didn't have to be elaborate, fancy, or even memorable.

As I write this, the average life expectancy in the US is 77 years. That's over 28,000 days. I wonder what percentage of those days people remember. It couldn't be many. Major events, good and bad, certainly have a chance to reserve space for memory recall. There are also random moments that seem to stick with you. Mostly, though, each day happens and is forgotten. That's not to say days are a waste. I believe experience and life's mini-journeys contribute to who we are, what we do, and inform our future behavior. As humans, we exist in a never-ending process of growth. For some, learning follows a traditional path to greater knowledge. For others, it's more primal and reinforcing––a guidepost for what to do and what not to do.

I've struggled with this and felt trapped in a cycle of expectations in which I always push myself to get better. I remember a coach of mine preaching, "You're either getting better or getting worse, but you're not staying the same." With that mindset, I rarely have felt settled. There always has been some mountain to climb. I'm not suggesting that striving for improvement is a bad thing. I'm just wondering how you can push yourself continuously to seek new heights and learn while also enjoying the simple things and moments.

I should have a better answer to this. Before her cancer, I saw mom grow and still retain her innate joy with life. I watched as she took courses to seek a college degree, improve her work skills, and sharpen her hobbies. Simultaneously, she did everything else expected of a mother and wife. What I never observed was her complaining or dreading what she had to do or her lot in life. She harbored a deep disappointment that she hadn't gone to college. As I've learned, dad and their courtship derailed that option. And yet, despite her missed chance at college, she relished both her family and the opportunity to try to achieve the goal of a college degree.

She also possessed the sweetest heart, content to embrace small moments and life with a sense of appreciation and grace. With these diary entries, I can feel her attempt to remind herself of the joy she felt with friends, family, tasks, hobbies, and living. It brings me comfort.

I'm also sad. As I've acknowledged, mom was my biggest fan, but she also wasn't afraid to point out when she thought I was getting a little too full of myself. She never hesitated to force me to slow down and enjoy life. I didn't fight her and tried to follow her lead. Most of the time, it worked. As I reflect on my life before her diagnosis and the subsequent battle that followed, there's no doubt I was happier when she was reminding me emotionally to find joy in all the right places.

It strikes me that in the waning days of September 1992, mom was attempting to maintain her positivity with a cloud looming over her head. These brief entries come in the few intervening days between chemo. Each reference to a moment of pleasure is followed by a reminder that, as she said, "the big C is coming." How brave it is to fight for who you are when you're being attacked.

However, I draw another conclusion from this. I'm so annoyed at myself for the daily stupidity I allow to enter my life and derail or hide the joys staring me in the face. How many days have I missed a chance to smile or laugh? Too many to count. Coach Jim Valvano said in his famous ESPY speech, days before he died from cancer, "To me, there are three things everyone should do every day. Number one is laugh. Number two is think––spend some time in thought. Number three, you should have your emotions move you to tears. If you laugh, think, and cry, that's a heck of a day."

I'd like to think I could embrace mom's ability to find happiness, or follow Valvano's lead about living each day before facing a death sentence. So far, I've failed at this. I have no doubt that had mom not developed cancer and had lived to her life expectancy (she would've been 77 this year), she would've hammered this perspective into me. After all, she had a way of getting me to accept her guidance.

However, that's not how it played out, and now I'm giving myself a second chance. My connection to her had faded, but her diary is beginning to sew the fabric back together.

### October 4, 1992

*Well, I am into my fourth day of chemo. So far, this time hasn't been as bad as before. I am beginning to get really bored here at home. Even though I feel a little sick and weak, I have done several household chores today. I just can't seem to get interested in "busy" work. I have finished the puzzles I was working on and the books I have, I just can't get into. I am very thankful that I am not as sick from the chemo as I was before. Very thankful. I am hopeful the shots don't bother me too much and keep my white count up. I guess I am just really anxious to try and get my life back to normal. The weekend wasn't a very good one when I think about all the rain and how depressing it was, but when I think about my reaction to chemo, it was a fabulous weekend. I am very thankful and anxious to get back to my normal everyday life and go back to work.*

### October 5, 1992

*I'm really sort of disappointed that the fatigue is hanging around a little longer than I thought it would. I don't really feel bad. I just don't have any evenings I want to do things, and I try, but my energy level is very low. I ran a few chores today (drugstore, cleaners, grocery), but when I came back, I was beat. I really want to do more because I am bored and because I can't rest at all at night. I am still very thankful for the lack of nausea. Mom and I took Andrew to the park. I was able to play with him just a little bit, but not much. I guess I just need to make up my mind that this is a slow process and quit worrying about it. I don't hurt anywhere, "Thank God." I just don't have any energy.*

### October 7, 1992

*Today has been a good day. Mom and I did a little housework this morning, then went to Ruth's, mom's hairdresser, S&S Cafeteria, Cloth Shop, Michaels, Waccamaw, then the drugstore. I feel good today. I bought things for Christmas, mostly things for crafts for Christmas. I also bought Christmas cards. I came home and addressed some of the cards. So, I'm ahead of the game for Christmas. Ray and I are ordering Chinese food for dinner.*

### October 8, 1992

*Today has been a very gloomy day. Rainy and dreary. I had lunch with Lisa at the Apple Cake Tea Room. It was really good for me to see her. I also ran errands (laundry and groceries). I also worked on some crafts. I did one of the hats I am going to give at Christmas. Ray has gone to his little league football game. I will be glad when this football season is over. It's amazing how the weather affects my mood. I can hardly stand it when it is dreary like this. It really depresses me.*

Mom is bored. Her mind is seeking activity, normalcy, life, but her body isn't so sure. She dreaded this round of chemo. Thankfully, those fears were unwarranted. However, the cumulative effects of her disease, surgery, chemo, and radiation are taking a toll.

Most of us need something to do. Sometimes it's no more than chores. However, beyond routine tasks, we need a broader sense of purpose and accomplishment. Our minds stay sharp when we seek to move forward. I think this is true regardless of your role in life. You don't have to be a leader or do transformative things to thrive by doing.

Mom enjoyed her job, her life, and how she contributed to making the world better for those she touched. Being unable to continue her life like before frustrated her, and it makes me wonder how I would react in a similar situation. How does anyone respond? I can't imagine sitting around and stewing over how I feel, what's going to happen next, what the doctors are going to say, or whether I am going to feel sick. It terrifies me to think I could or would spend so much time stuck in my head, alone with my thoughts.

And yet, maybe that's exactly what I'd do. Maybe I wouldn't have the gumption to march on, seemingly mindless of my reality. Maybe fatigue would rule the day, and I'd fail to find the physical or emotional strength to function as close to normal as possible. Who knows?

Someday, I'm likely to find out. Unless I die suddenly, or by accident, I'll likely learn that I have some dreadful disease, with some awful treatment that alters my lifestyle. Then I'll face what mom faced––boredom, anxiety, loneliness––a world driven by thinking and not doing.

A myriad of self-help books are available on what to do with your time or hobbies you could pick up. It all sounds so encouraging––and awful. Mom loved writing notes, doing puzzles, running errands, and reading, but most of all, she loved being active. Sadly, her body was pushing back when she got active. It meant she was left to exist cerebrally, and the dominating thought that never left her mind was cancer.

It's no wonder that the word "depressed" has appeared in her diary entries, as well as mentions of how the weather influences her mood. Her mind and focus are narrowing. There wasn't that much to think about.

On some level, I could see this happening, and I didn't

offer any meaningful help. My mindset was always to lean forward; therefore, I didn't know how to interact with her. After the diagnosis, talking with her and spending time together were different. We didn't talk about the future unless it was some pending treatment or doctor's appointment. We no longer talked about trips, family gatherings, her favorite sports teams, or her family and their happenings. Life had become a repeat of the daily grind and the fear of what was next.

It was during this time that mom's attitude began to change. It was the beginning of a cycle of isolation that, although subtle at first, would become a defining feature of who she was. This once gregarious, happy, optimistic person became driven by what was in her headspace, the tightrope of a depressive personality, and her dependence on medications.

# CHAPTER 5

**October 28, 1992**

*I haven't written in a long time, but the last three weeks have been very good and busy. I have had a visit from both my granddaughters. They are both good babies, and they are beautiful. I had a wonderful time with them, and I got really close to them. Their eyes would light up when they saw nana. That makes me feel great. I have also worked hard at getting my strength back. Housework, shopping, etc. I have thought at times during the past three weeks that maybe I should have gone back to work earlier, but now I know I made the right decision. I had chemo yesterday, and actually, I feel pretty good. This is the best I have ever felt after chemo. We'll see what the Neupogen does when I start the shots today. I am really looking forward*

*to going back to work on Monday. I have several*
*days to get ready—the house, my clothes, finish up*
*letters and Christmas cards and maybe even think*
*about some Christmas presents. It's going to be good*
*to see everyone at work.*

G RANDBABIES ARE INDESCRIBABLY WONDERFUL. As a new papaw, I can confirm there's nothing better. It changes your perspective, provides an unconditional bond that's hard to convey, and brings a feeling of accomplishment to your later years. Time spent with your children's children is special.

For mom, Ashley and Brittany, born within a few months of each other, gave her the little girls she never had. She wasted no time being the doting nana, and she was great at it. Watching mom with her grandkids was everything you would've expected.

When the cancer surfaced, her interactions with the kids changed. Mom became more childlike. She couldn't hold the babies anymore or pick them up, so she got down on the floor with them. Nana would lie on the ground and make eye contact on their level. She would take their toys and build stories around the stuffed items. It didn't matter what the character was—whether it was Simba from *Lion King* or Barney. Whatever grabbed the girls' attention became the basis for a pretend story.

And yes, they looked at her with wonder. The light in their eyes was only matched by the spark in mom's eyes. They were spellbound together, lost in imagination, and laughing with pure joy. Nana was a creative storyteller. She was raised around kinfolk who found entertainment in spinning a good tale. It was natural to her. Reliving her time on the floor with the kids is one of my favorite memories of mom. It captured her heritage, her loving soul, and her spirit.

This time was also an escape for mom, an outlet that allowed her to cast away dark thoughts and connect with a vibrant extension of herself. Mom's time with the girls, and later my son, were special and needed.

Neither Rick nor I lived close by, so we didn't do this enough. I'd bet we saw her four or five times a year. Looking back, that was a mistake. I don't know how I could've altered this, but I should've. We needed to see her monthly. It would've been hard, but life is hard when you're working on a career, a marriage, and raising kids. Nevertheless, that isn't a good excuse.

It's about priorities, and we set priorities. If you let it, life will consume you and dictate your day, attitude, and actions. Before you know it, it's been weeks since you visited with family, and schedules fill up.

I always have felt guilty about not being there enough. I'm disappointed I wasn't holding her hand or kissing her forehead during the most brutal of times. I should've been there more, but that wasn't my greatest failure. My biggest mistake wasn't engaging in normal moments—times when there wasn't a crisis. She would've benefited so much from those little girls being around—the story time and the pretend moments when everything had a happy ending.

I wasn't emotionally present during her journey—too busy chasing silly dreams. I should've been ensuring that mom had time to be nana.

### March 4, 1994

*I started back to work on November 1, 1992. It was really good to be back. I managed to work and just take off a few days when I had chemo. I wanted to work and keep going. During this time frame, I was starting to have trouble with my stomach. Because of ignorance about cancer, I was afraid I had stomach cancer. Finally, shortly before Christmas, I went to Dr. Barnett. He said he was sure I had gallstones. A few tests verified this because my gall bladder was so inflamed. I had to have surgery immediately, so I had surgery four days before Christmas. Fortunately, I had finished my Christmas shopping. Rick, Rebecca, and Brittany came the day before Christmas. We had a very good time. We didn't have the traditional Christmas dinner. The kids bought groceries, and we grilled steaks. It was great.*

*Because I had gall bladder surgery and was taking chemo, I could not return to work until March 1993. Things went smoothly from March until August. I noticed a large tennis ball-shaped spot on my stomach above and to the right of my navel. A visit to Dr. Vickers revealed that this was a hernia, and this meant more surgery again.*

*I recovered from the surgery pretty quick and*

*returned to work. During all this time, I had been having trouble with my joints, especially my knees and my right hip. I would visit Dr. Bell (ortho-pedist), and he would put cortisone shots in my knees and sometimes my hip. The X-rays revealed nothing except arthritis.*

After reading this much of mom's diary, I'm now resigned to the fact that mom didn't broadly journal her thoughts. Her entries seem event-driven and focused exclusively on her physical health. Nothing wrong with that. I'm assuming she thought of this diary as her outlet for things related to her disease.

I shouldn't be surprised that mom catalogued her feelings about her disease in writing and didn't memo-rialize other aspects of her life. Mom was too outgoing to be alone with her pen and her thoughts. For her, life was to be shared.

And boy did she share. My childhood memories center around a full house. Whether it was neighbors, family, mom and dad's friends, my friends, Rick's friends, UT football players, fellow church members, and even strang-ers that mom or dad randomly met. The house always was busting at the seams, and mom always was cooking.

She could throw together the heartiest meal in record time and create the biggest mess you've ever seen. It was a sight to witness and a joy to eat. Mom cherished bringing smiles to people's faces and loved to over-serve. Once everyone was stuffed, mom wanted to talk and laugh. She had a way of making you feel special. She would smile at you, look you in the eye, and listen intently to what you had to say. Because of her ability to connect personally, people felt like they'd known her forever.

Dad was the same way. He loved to have people around, all kinds of people. Our house was diverse before diversity was cool. It didn't matter to mom or dad what your background was, where you came from, who you knew, what color your skin was, if you were rich or poor. They just liked people, and they liked making them smile.

After I moved away, mom and dad grew their network of friends and continued to expand the number of people they impacted. When I went home, I always was introduced to someone new who spoke of my parents like they'd known them forever.

These memories always stuck with me. It was a happy household filled with love, compassion, and acceptance. Then it stopped.

Cancer didn't just take mom's life; it took away how she lived. I've tried hard to recall a time after she had cancer when mom or dad welcomed people the way they did before, but I can't. A pall had fallen over the house, and even when they tried to replicate the old haphazard gatherings, they couldn't. I'm sure there were times they tried, and they weren't feeling up to it. More likely, though, the people who were there acted differently. I know I did. No longer was it OK to have mom frantically work in the kitchen; she needed to "let everyone else do that." The play's director was silenced. After all, she was sick and should rest while we "took care of things."

This drove mom crazy, and it affected dad. He was

a primary caregiver, and he loved mom, but he missed the world they'd created. Although he didn't get bitter, he became more subdued.

Together, and in their own way, they felt the sting of this life-altering diagnosis. Without a plan or guidance, they became beholden to the disease's power. I'm sure they assumed this time would pass, mom would get better, and all would return to normal. It didn't. Cancer never left their minds, mom never regained her defining spirit, and the opportunity to maintain and defend the life they enjoyed passed.

Those of us who lived outside of the home shared in this failure to recreate joyful gatherings. The joy mom felt when she hosted was the joy her guests expressed. Admittedly, that's hard to do when you feel sadness. It's tough to feel free to laugh, play, goof off, and relax when you're keenly aware your host is ill. It seems disrespectful. For me, I couldn't shake how sad I felt every time I saw her. I couldn't allow myself to be carefree. I just couldn't. I feel weak admitting that, but it's true. All these years later, I don't know how to characterize how I felt when I looked at her. All I can admit is that something held me back.

I don't know the right answer or continuum for how to act when you're visiting someone who's sick. Certainly, she no longer could whip up a dinner and host on a whim like before, but she wasn't bedridden. I think we might have treated her like she was.

Her diary entries suggest no obvious clues to my reaction, and on the surface, offer little insight into how

I feel as a write this. However, I know what's coming, and I'm angry with myself for allowing a diagnosis whose outcome was still uncertain to influence my behavior as though the die was cast, and we were just waiting it out.

I know mom enjoyed Christmas with Rick, and I'm sure she thought the steaks were great, but deep down, she would've loved to put on a memorable spread for her family while depositing flour in crevices throughout the kitchen that would only be found in the spring.

PART II

# CHAPTER 6

### March 4, 1994, Cont.

*In September 1993, I was due to have a precautionary test for cancer. I had a bone scan, liver, lungs, and brain scan. Everything was OK, and all of us were so happy. One year later, and nothing had recurred. My tumor marker was staying in the 30s and 40s. This was a little high, but Dr. Kerns thought this might be normal for me.*

*During the next few months, the pain increased in my hip. I could hardly walk. A November tumor marker revealed an elevated tumor marker (48). Nothing drastic, but enough to worry me. I wanted another test done. This time, it jumped to 73, and Dr. Kerns was concerned. He ordered a repeat of all the tests.*

*One week before Christmas, on a rainy Friday,*

*Ray and I went to Dr. Kerns' office. I had a "hot spot" in my hip. Further tests were needed to determine exactly what was going on, but it was suspicious. That Friday night, I called my friend, Dr. Barnett, to find out what he thought. His response to the radiology report was "Do you want to know the truth?" I said of course I do. He said it was very bad news and that the cancer had probably returned. The following Monday, Ray and I went to see Dr. Bell. He did a simple little X-ray, and there it was. Ray and I could see it very plainly. It involved about one-third to half of the flat-shaped bone in my pelvic area. We were in complete shock. Dr. Bell answered as many of our questions as he could. We found out that recurrent breast cancer is incurable, that the prognosis is not good (10% to 20% of women survive five years). We left his office on a rainy, dreary night really scared and afraid.*

TODAY, ROUGHLY 30% OF THE women who are diagnosed with metastatic breast cancer survive five years. However, on average, most women only survive three years. Metastatic breast cancer remains incurable. It can be treated, but sadly, if you have it, you're not getting rid of it. Despite 30 years of research, the prognosis is still bad.

I don't recall knowing how dangerous a recurrence of the cancer could be. Mom frequently shared her fear that it would come back. Each time she spoke of her worry, I remember thinking that her concerns were more related to having to endure more uncomfortable treatment, not that a recurrence was the beginning of the end. It seems stupid to me that I was so clueless. I can't explain why when I first learned mom had cancer, I didn't educate myself on breast cancer and the long-term risks she faced. Obviously, my knowledge level wouldn't have altered the outcome, but why had I avoided seeking answers?

Based on the above diary entry, it's not even clear to me that mom previously understood what a recurrence meant to her future. She seems to suggest that she learned about the survival rate once it had returned. I would've thought she would've asked the doctors in the beginning.

At the end of the 20th century, the relationship between healthcare providers and patients was different. Doctors regularly kept information to themselves. Even when mom asked her primary care physician, who was her friend, what this meant, he was hesitant to tell her. Without the Internet or a doctor offering the information, learning mortality statistics on a given disease required significant time, effort, and likely some basic clinical knowledge to decode the highly technical clinical trials that were published. It was daunting and, therefore, unreasonable to expect most patients to do this on their own.

Getting educated on your diagnosis and options is hard, but I'm not sure that the difficulty in gathering information is the primary barrier to a patients' understanding of what they face. More likely, this was still the era when patients trusted that their doctors would tell them what they needed to know. And doctors weren't always open. My sense is that they thought they were helping the patient. After all, who wants to know they're going to die?

I recently spoke with a dear friend who was told his cancer had returned and metastasized. He seemed cheerful and almost nonchalant about what was to come. I carefully asked him what the prognosis was, hoping his mood reflected good news. He responded, "I don't know, and I'm not asking the doctor because he doesn't know either." As our phone conversation continued, I quickly Googled to see whether I could find the statistics on life expectancy and outlook in his case. My heart sank as I saw that most patients lived between six months and two years. Did he know and just wasn't telling me, or was he oblivious to reality? I honestly don't know and didn't push the point. I told him I loved him and made a note that I needed to go see him.

Maybe not wanting to know is a default for some people. When mom was first diagnosed, I think she fit into that group. She didn't want to know what could happen, and obviously neither did I. If we had wanted, we were both stubborn enough that either we would've forced the doctors to tell us, or we would've committed the time to conduct research and get smart.

Mom possessed a dominant ability to be optimistic, and she taught me the same mindset. My birth defect? No problem. Mom knew how to march forward and wasn't interested in languishing in what was. She wanted to believe in what was going to be, what could happen. I believe she didn't ask about the what-ifs because she believed it was going to be OK.

Maybe her positivity, along with my friend's, is the best way to live, to hope. Why let details and statistics get in the way of your own personal vision? I can see that. However, I don't know whether I'd feel the same way. I've come to believe in life that hope is a lousy strategy. Acceptance of the truth feels like a better approach, but that's arrogant for me to claim. I haven't faced what mom did, nor what my friend is facing. How the hell do I know what I'd do?

Understanding mom's optimism always included a never-ending battle with her fear of the unknown. On one hand, she believed in possibilities, while on the other, the cancer was back, and her doctor told her there wasn't much hope. All she could do was fight for more time.

The world is full of inspirational stories of people who are given a death diagnosis and somehow find a way to make their remaining time meaningful and impactful. It's encouraging but is it a reasonable expectation? I think it has to do with finding a purpose for existing, a reason for suffering. Viktor Frankl wrote in *Man's Search for Meaning*, "We must never forget that we may also find meaning in life even when confronted with a hopeless situation, when facing a fate that cannot be changed. For what then matters is to bear witness to the uniquely human potential at its best, which is transform a personal tragedy into a triumph, to turn one's predicament into a human achievement. When we are no longer able to change a situation—just think of an incurable disease, such as inoperable cancer—we are challenged to change ourselves."

Frankl is suggesting that humans can elevate themselves during a time of despair. I don't believe he's arguing that everyone should or will. I think he's saying it's possible. However, just because it's possible doesn't mean an observer has the right to expect anything close to personal achievement during strife from a sick loved one. We can't and shouldn't judge another person's situation, nor their reaction to it. No one has the right to determine what an individual's purpose is, or what their reason is for enduring. It's the most personal of decisions, and I believe in the sacred pact that the suffering make with themselves and the God they believe in.

Because it's so personal, and often not shared, those around the sick individual sometimes fail to understand the rationale for decisions. As I look back, I realize that this was an inflection point. From this moment forward in mom's journey, I was confused. I never understood why she fought so hard. If she internalized the statistics, what was she doing?

In the winter of 1993, she had no idea what was coming. She was preparing to fight, but I'm not sure whether she could've told me why.

I've accepted that it didn't matter why she did what she did. It wasn't my place to question or wonder. I, like too many men, am a fixer. When I see something wrong, I want to fix it. I want to work through the problem, find the best answer, and put my head down and execute. As such, at times, I failed to listen, to internalize what's in front of me. It doesn't matter that mom didn't have all the answers. She faced death—a death that was unpredictable in its time, physical costs, and emotional toll. The only absolute was that she was going to die.

### *March 4, 1994, Cont.*

*I had an MRI, and on Thursday talked to Dr. Kerns about treatment. His initial thoughts were radiation and large doses of chemo.*

*Ray and I had planned to go see Tennessee play in the Citrus Bowl and go to Disney World. Dr. Kerns said to go on and try to have a good time, and we would start treatment when I returned. We went through the motions of Christmas and went on our trip. Some parts were fun. The pain, even with painkillers, was tremendous, and in the back of our minds was the cancer. We probably should have stayed home.*

*While we were in Florida, I decided I wanted to be aggressive with the cancer and not let it slowly kill me. I wanted more than one opinion. Mike made an appointment with the cancer specialist at UAB. I thought maybe a bone marrow transplant would cure this cancer immediately. On the Monday after New Year's, I visited Dr. Barnett early in the morning to tell him what I wanted to do. He said it was OK to be aggressive, just go to the right place, and the right place was Duke University. He contacted Dr. Kerns, who contacted Duke. At that point, they thought the best treatment was just radiation.*

*So, during the month of January, I took 16 treatments of radiation at Thompson Cancer Survival Center. I continued to work during these treatments, which left me very fatigued.*

*The radiation helped the pain in my hips somewhat. After radiation, the pain started coming back slowly.*

It seems so random. Were the physicians following an accepted protocol? Did the medical community even have an accepted standard of care for how to treat metastatic breast cancer? I don't know, but I doubt they did. Mom wanted to be aggressive and mentioned a bone marrow transplant. Her local doctor suggests radiation and chemo, and the "best teaching hospital" countered with radiation only.

Medicine is science-based, but it's also an art of elimination. Sometimes a diagnosis isn't obvious, and the only way the clinician determines what's happening is through a process to eliminate what isn't happening. That's a rational approach, and the medical community has ample diagnostic tools to find the answer. In the case of cancer, diagnosis isn't generally the challenge. The hard part is knowing what to do.

With the benefit of today's information, cancer treatment 30 years ago seems like a game of educated guessing, and that's not unreasonable. Physicians decided what to do based on the facts as they knew them, their experience, and any available clinical research. Unfortunately, what was available to guide doctors didn't offer good answers. As a result, in this case, and likely most cases, it appears they were trying things and hoping.

It's frustrating to consider what's happening when a patient like mom is embarking on a treatment regimen. Without question, time is of the essence. Every moment you're not killing the cancer, it's growing and killing you. It's a race. You cannot waste a day. And yet, when you begin treatment, you've allotted weeks, or months, for that strategy, hoping the balance of dying cells has shifted to the cancer losing and the patient gaining the upper hand.

To make matters worse, the patient pays a heavy price for enduring cancer treatments. All cancer treatments damage the patient. Whether it's damage to their body, their mind, or their spirit, patients initially come out of cancer treatments diminished. If they're lucky, it works. If not, they move on to the next treatment. In the interim, valuable time has been lost, and the patient is weaker. Cancer has won this battle and is now closer to winning the war.

I'm not placing blame. I want to believe, and so I will, that the clinicians did their best. Mom had metastatic breast cancer, and nothing was going to change her fate. What could've been different were the decisions that were made, combined with a better understanding of those choices' implications. Mom wanted to be aggressive, got two opinions, and did what they said. I don't believe she understood her options and what she reasonably should've expected.

It's widely accepted today that patients need an advocate to help them navigate complex diseases. In the early '90s, no one used that phrase. Healthcare was just beginning to understand patient rights and communication. Mom needed someone to help her process what was happening. Dad wasn't the answer, and neither was her mom. I failed her. I was present, but only part-time.

I'm probably naïve to think a better-informed, critical-thinking-based approach would've made the remainder of mom's life better, but I still do. So many choices that were made led to unintended consequences that conflicted with why she was fighting.

I don't believe in revisionist history. There's no way to know how you would react in the moment, faced with all the emotion of that time. You can't change what's happened. You only can learn from it. I don't get a do-over, nor does mom. This makes me sad, but it also makes me committed to be there, if I'm needed in the future, for any friend or loved one. It's the least I can do.

### *March 4, 1994, Cont.*

*During the next month or so, mom started feeling really bad. I knew she was worrying herself to death about me. After some tests, it was determined she had heart problems. A heart surgeon put her in the hospital and did angioplasty surgery. She had problems with hallucinations in the CCU, and Dr. Barnett suggested that she and I both see a psychiatrist.*

*Mom has responded well to the rehabilitation. She goes three times a week to Fort Sanders West for exercise, classes on nutrition, etc. She has lost 29 pounds. The psychiatrist has helped her with depression. She is a completely different person. She is happy, she goes out more, she is going to church every Sunday, and she goes out with her friend Ralph. This makes me very happy. I did not want her to grieve over me.*

When you lose someone, it's hard to believe you will ever remember your loved one without feeling pain and sadness. Fortunately, in my experience, there comes a time when your memories become joyful again, and the good times dominate your thoughts. With each death of a family member, I slowly have cast aside the heartbreak and found myself consumed with only happy memories. It's a blessing that passing days allow you to find peace and comfort.

Reading mom's diary and writing about it obviously requires focusing on the worst of times, and this renewal of pain has been emotional and difficult. Frankly, it's exhausting, and despite my commitment to get through her words, I've grown worried that my memories of life before her cancer are fading. Several times, I've tried to channel the happy feelings I had before I opened up mom's diary, to no avail.

However, the above passage brings a huge grin to my face and, thus, a flood of good feelings. As people, sometimes we hear what we want to hear, or in this case, read what we want to read. Nevertheless, the above passage reminds me of the gift I received being kin to mom and mamaw.

Where I come from, mom and mamaw could best be described as a hoot. Five parts sugar and one part pepper. They were funny, sometimes with cute phrases or sharp tongues.

Mamaw's family used humor to accept whatever circumstances they faced. A harmless practical joke was always in the works. Family gatherings weren't loud, and alcohol wasn't present. For them, a competitive watermelon-seed-spitting contest, touch football, or horseshoes were all the entertainment they needed before it was time to eat. And boy did they eat. Fried chicken, meatloaf, pork barbecue, hot dogs, hamburgers, and casseroles of every kind anchored the menu. Vegetables from the garden, fresh or canned from the previous year, were shared in abundance. And yes, mac and cheese is a vegetable. All this topped off with desserts. Mamaw's family loved desserts. They loved making them and eating them. Cobblers, pies, cakes, and banana pudding, served with ice cream, completed every gathering. To eat heartily with family was a centerpiece of mamaw's life.

Her passion for fixing food and gathering family filled her life with joy and hope. It was a beautiful way to extract every ounce of happiness out of life that didn't have a lot of big things to look forward to.

Then it was story time.

Mom always loved to tell of the tradition that mamaw's brothers started to welcome new young men to the family.

For whatever reason, mom's uncles thought it would be appropriate to wrestle the new in-law to the ground and bite their ear till it bled. Not sure what that says about the family, but it was funny. Dad received this high-class welcome, as did Karen's husband. I remember seeing this happen once as a child. I laughed so hard, likely because I knew it was going to happen to me. I was blood.

The latest practical joke played on one of the brothers was always a favorite topic after supper. There was the time Uncle Alton, the baby of the clan, got the best of Uncle James, his much older brother. Uncle James was proud of his garden. He loved to harvest the vegetables and can anything he didn't consume that summer. As such, one year, he planted 30 tomato plants, expecting a big bounty. Early in the season, James went out of town for three days. He couldn't wait to get back and see how the garden looked. Imagine his surprise, and concern, when he returned and was told by his neighbor how Alton had come over each morning and dutifully watered his plants. That sounded like a loving gesture, but it also sounded fishy. Wasting not a second, James ran to his garden and carefully inspected every plant to see what had happened. To his dismay, everything looked great. The plants were perfect. It wasn't until they began to produce tomatoes that the reality of what happened become obvious.

On the first night James was out of town, with nothing but the moon to light the field, Alton pulled up every tomato plant and planted tommy toe tomatoes. James wasn't amused. It's not much fun, nor practical, to can cherry tomatoes. Alton wasn't being mean; they loved each other and had been joshing back and forth for decades. They were both grandpas when this happened.

The jokes and stories never ended. It was a way of life. When I was a kid, I loved mamaw and her family, and the joy I felt watching people giggle and act silly. As an adult, I respect how they lived. They came from a tough background and never had anything given to them, and yet, they loved life, family, and the joy of spreading happiness to whomever they met.

Mom grew up in this world, and she brought the same care and enthusiasm to her life as a wife and mother. She would prepare a spread like it was a family gathering, and if the family wasn't around, her and dad would invite people over to enjoy the fun.

Mom could make sloppy joes for a group, and everyone would feel like they'd been given a feast. She put extra doses of love into everything she cooked. Unfortunately, she didn't leave behind recipes. For years, I searched for evidence that she wrote down the secrets to the dishes she prepared. Sadly, I've concluded that she only used experience, love, and whatever ingredients she had.

I don't remember her dishes being heavy on spices. I don't think I learned what curry was until I went to college, but it didn't matter because her meals were memorable and plentiful. When I recall the amount of food I ate growing up, I'm amazed I wasn't huge. It was a different time—there wasn't as much processed food, and we never sat down long enough to let calories settle. We were always on the move, looking for something to do or play.

Like her relatives, mom loved a good joke. I distinctly remember dad's 30th birthday party. The house was full of friends, and laughter dominated every conversation. It was a joyous time. As we finished off a large meal, mom slipped away. Shortly thereafter, she rounded the corner with a big cake lit with glowing candles. Her face was beaming. She placed the cake on the table and stepped aside so dad could blow out the candles. As he peered down, he lost it. He burst out laughing. The cake read "Happy Birthday, Noassitol." It didn't take long for the room to get in on the joke, and everyone took their turns pointing out that dad didn't have a butt that could fill any pair of pants. Mom and dad smiled from ear to ear. I can still feel the energy. It was a memorable moment in my life.

It was also a time when the world you lived in felt sheltered. For me, I thought everyone lived like we did. We didn't travel much, and when we did, we always went to Jekyll Island, Georgia, for one week. It wasn't until I got to college that I realized the world was wildly different and that there were lots of ways people lived. I'm OK with the fact that I was raised with a small-town mindset, by small-town people. Nothing wrong with living peacefully in your own world. Over the years, I've learned to love the diversity and uniqueness that this planet has to offer, but I'm never far away from the simple, comfortable days as a child living in a world dominated by the love of mom, dad, and mamaw. In fact, I'd give anything for a bowl of mom's banana pudding.

# CHAPTER 7

*March 24, 1994*

*Ray had another joint replacement on his right knee for the third time. It was a horrible operation lasting 7½ hours on the operating table. He had some really bad times in the hospital due to an allergic reaction to medicine. I stayed with him in the hospital every night and most days. He is home now doing rehabilitation. He is doing quite well, although his pain is still there.*

DAD WAS A TOUGH GUY. Not a big guy, and not aggressive or violent, just sturdy. But there was scar tissue he carried with him from his childhood. He didn't talk about it, but you could tell there was always something missing in his story. When I was young,

I wondered about how he was able to rise out of the environment he was raised in. Neither his parents nor his grandmother were warm, charming people. I don't know how many times he was told he was loved.

Against this backdrop, he joined the Army and quickly thereafter met mom. He told me that everything good that ever happened to him began once he met her, and he loved her passionately. His unwavering commitment to building a life with mom was obvious. He found his life partner, but there was more to it. Dad lived his life always committed to doing better than his history. He didn't carry a chip on his shoulder, trying to prove something to someone. It was more of an unyielding commitment to building a life that he could be proud of.

He, like all of us, had faults. He was demanding and at times had a temper that came from out of nowhere. As a young child, I didn't know why he reacted the way he did. By the time I went to college, I began to understand him and to accept the fact that he was doing everything in his life without the benefit of an adult role model. We're all imperfect. Life is hard, but it's more difficult when you're plowing ground you've never tilled before.

I watched dad exceed his own capabilities and expectations, as well as love mom unconditionally. And I watched him find joy in being told he was loved.

In return, he showed his love and support in ways that he hadn't received from his family. Despite being reared in a cycle of dysfunction, he created an environment for Rick and me that catapulted us into the lives we lived.

Dad worked hard at his job, and also to be in our

lives. He wouldn't miss a game we were playing and was involved in our activities. Even though at the time, he seemed intense about us succeeding in sports, I learned, as time passed, that his love for us wasn't about how we did on the field. He wanted us to compete, to prepare for a world that expects you to fight for what you have. His approach worked, and we learned valuable lessons from him.

I also learned how to endure pain and get on with it. Dad hurt his knee while stationed in Germany in the mid-'60s. The military surgeon botched the procedure, and he was shipped to Walter Reed Hospital, where he stayed for nine months. They wanted to fuse his knee, but he refused.

He eventually rehabbed the knee and finished his military service with a damaged joint. His injury led to a lifetime of knee problems. Mom references his third joint replacement. He would ultimately have six replacements and over 20 surgeries in his life. He was in constant pain, but never stopped moving.

He was obsessed with keeping things tidy, wanting the house clean and the yard perfect. I used to think he was over the top or influenced by his military service, but I was wrong. Several years ago, I was teasing him about constantly mowing the lawn, even when he wasn't physically capable. His response was matter of fact: "Mike, I learned a long time ago that no matter what your situation is, you can take care of what you have. Even if you're poor, you can mow the grass." There it was: He lived his life never forgetting where he came from. He was going to love mom and his boys like he'd never been loved, be there for his friends, be proud without being prideful, and––dammit––he was going to mow the lawn even when it didn't need it.

### *April 24, 1994*

*For the past two weeks, I have been doing what four doctors have suggested. Stay home and rest. My hip is better. I got to the point where I had to walk with a cane. My cancer situation is in limbo. There is some question as to whether it is back in my hip or not. Rest, anti-inflammatory drugs, then a test will determine that. For me, cancer is like sports: Extreme highs, but mostly extreme lows. Living with the fact that I have incurable cancer is really hard. I think about it all the time when my mind is not busy. I really have a big cloud over my head. There are lots of unknowns, but things I do know are that recurrent breast cancer is incurable, and that women with recurrent breast cancer only have a 10% to 20% chance to survive five years. It will return in your bones, lungs, or brain. Living with these facts is very difficult. You live from test to test and pain to pain. One thing that is improving with the help of Dr. Demers is the guilt I have about my cancer. I feel guilty about worrying my family, and my family does. I feel guilty about the fact that my co-workers are having to pick up the load. I feel mad because I can't work at home and do my part. I don't think I will ever get to the point where*

*I don't fear cancer and the things it does to you.*

*I realize that I have to lift some of the burden from my shoulders, and I am trying. I know I should think about Pat, which is very hard for me. I have taken that first step by staying home these past two weeks. I did not realize how bad I felt until I started feeling better. In the past few days, I have wondered why I let myself get so rundown and kept going in spite of the pain. I know taking time off was the right thing to do, but when I talk to people at work, I feel very guilty. They tell me to do what is best for Pat, and they mean it.*

*The past two weeks have done something else. Since Ray is still off from work because of his knee surgery, we have had some really good time together. We rode in the convertible over the Dogwood Trails and on some small jaunts. More than anything, though, we have talked and talked and talked. This has really been helpful to us, even though we have been married almost 30 years. We still learn more about each other every day. I am very lucky to have him. He truly loves me even with all of my problems.*

I've reread this entry several times over the past few days and found myself unsure what to say. Processing her diary is challenging; her thoughts about guilt are tough for me. On one hand, I'm frustrated that she would feel any guilt about how she's impacting those she loves. It seems so unnecessary. I remember knowing how she worried about us too much. I didn't know it dominated her thinking.

On the other hand, I understand how she came to this place. Presumably, each person has something in their life that drives them, gives them pleasure, or is the source of their passion or happiness. For mom, it was taking care of everyone. When mom was healthy, I thought she was driven by other motivations, maybe bigger motivations. She wasn't. Everything in her life revolved around her desire to give.

I'm not being critical. When she was able, mom found joy in her life providing joy for others. It worked for her. Until it didn't.

It would be disingenuous for me to pass judgment. I have my own version of wanting to make people happy, and it has been a challenge for the past 35 years. As I've grown older, I've accepted that many, if not most, of the struggles I've faced professionally have come as a result of wanting to meet or exceed others' expectations. Frankly, I'm crushed when I feel I've disappointed someone.

My motivation isn't a need to be liked or an insecurity that manifests itself as someone constantly seeking approval or affirmation. Rather, it's a very personal, internal desire to provide value, happiness, or success to those with whom I interact. I think, like mom did, that it's a noble goal to want to make others feel good. It's just an unreasonable way to live.

Since my career began, I've made decisions that I don't believe reflected what I wanted, but were made with some concern for what I thought others wanted or expected. I was married during my final year of college. Tiffiny's family was very different from mine. As a result, I felt pressure—some external and some of my own doing—to excel at what they valued. In some respects, I became like dad, convinced I needed to do better than where I came from. Simply put, I felt pressure to succeed under the parameters of how my in-laws judged success. As such, I made career decisions that, in hindsight, weren't what I wanted. Unfortunately, once this starts, it's hard to change course. For some time now, I've felt that I lived a life that wasn't what I would've chosen if I'd put my personal desires first.

Mom says she knows she needs to think about herself first, but she said it's hard. Obviously, it was for her, and it was for me too. Acknowledging the challenge of putting yourself at the front of the line is an important step, but it doesn't ensure happiness. You have to live the life that best fits you.

If I'm being honest, one of my primary goals of reading mom's diary was to try and understand whether she was happy in the life she had before cancer, or felt like she hadn't done what she wanted. Mom was smart, driven to learn, and an achiever. I mentioned earlier that I was aware mom had things in her life that she wanted to do, but never was able to pursue them. Did this bother her? Did she have regrets? I have no doubt she loved dad and being a mom, and I couldn't imagine her not filling that role, but many aspects to her weren't nourished.

I began this process hoping and believing that the unvarnished truth would present itself. After all, when you're facing death, it's time to get real. However, I perceive her innate sense of responsibility overriding any reflection or regrets. She may not have had any. Maybe she wouldn't have changed anything, or else the weight of thinking about a terminal disease was so heavy on her mind that she couldn't or wouldn't rehash her life or the what-ifs.

My interest in this subject is borne of the realization that I'm so like mom. She was such a strong presence in my life from day one. I found comfort in her and a foundation on which I could grow. Recently, I've begun to reconsider my life, decisions, and how I made them. I've recognized that I can't change the past, and that I don't want to live in a constant state of regret. However, to my knowledge, I'm healthy and, thus, lucky. There's time. Unlike mom, I have the opportunity to explore these thoughts without impending death hanging over me.

I now recognize that this book isn't just about mom's journey, but also about me and my life. I guess that makes sense, as the interconnectivity was bound to present itself. It had to. I'm seeking a reconnection with mom, a chance to delve into our relationship and explore how her DNA influences me. It has been so long since I spoke to her––since she smiled at me and provided counsel, compassion, empathy, or a simple hug. I miss her, as she was someone who understood me.

I don't know whether I'll ever learn what mom felt about how she lived her life. Maybe she did exactly what she wanted. I hope so. I know I haven't, but I'm at peace, and I'm grateful. I have a gift––the gift of time, connection, and opportunity. Mom isn't here, but her words and presence are piercing my body, and I'm once again reminded that it's OK to be me.

### *April 25, 1994*

*Well, the last 24 hours have not been that good. Last night, I began to feel congested with a sore throat and earache. The worst part about that is I didn't sleep well at all. I was up and down all night. That meant lots of time to think and worry. The middle of the night is a horrible time to think. Right now, I am very concerned about the way my hip feels. I may be doing a little too much activity, but basically, I am taking it easy. It's impossible for me to get this cancer off my mind when the pain is always there. Mom planted the garden today. My <u>grand</u> contribution was watering the plants.*

*Dear God, I pray that if I cannot be healed of this cancer that you grant me some relief from this pain. Please help me keep a positive attitude so I will not drag my family into the depressed state I'm feeling now. Help all of us be strong and help me set the example. Please help all of our friends from church—Libba, Kevin, and all the sick and the shut-ins. Thank you for my wonderful family and the success you have brought my boys. Please be with Ray as he deals with my illness, as well as his mom. Also be with him as he deals with his job and please grant him some success in both his Sam's Club adventure and the import business. We just want to be able to put the financial burden on the*

*back burner with all of our medical problems. Dear*
*God, thank you for always listening and caring. I*
*would like to be healed from this terrible disease,*
*but if that is not your will, please help me to handle*
*all of the problems and emotional feelings that come*
*with it. Please help me be strong and keep a smile*
*on my face. Especially to give you all the praise in*
*Jesus' name. Amen.*

In the late 1950s, mom's dad co-founded the Free
Will Baptist Church on Detroit Avenue. Uncle James,
mamaw's older brother, traveled from Middle Tennessee
to Knoxville to lay the bricks for the church building. A
few years after the church was built, the University of
Tennessee absorbed all the properties on Detroit Avenue,
forcing the congregation to move to South Knoxville.
A new building was erected, and service resumed. The
modest, red-brick church was a staple of mom's childhood
and holds a small place in my mind. For a young boy,
it was intimidating, but I think most people viewed
it as a welcoming environment in which to worship.
Lasting memories were created in the still-standing
country church. It's where Aunt Karen married Levourn,
a wedding I vaguely remember, and I was baptized there.
I don't have any recollection of the moment I was dunked
in the water.

For the first few years of my life, the growing West
family attended papaw's church. By the time I was seven,
we moved to West Knoxville and began to search for a
new place to worship. I remember several attempts at

trying out nearby Baptist churches. I don't know why, but none of them stuck. In time, we visited Concord Presbyterian Church, a beautiful white-framed building with a historic steeple that sat across the railroad tracks from Fort Loudon Lake. Years later, it reminds me of countless churches I've seen in small towns across New England. However, in the late '70s, I wouldn't have said that. I'd never been north of LaFollette, Tennessee.

With mom as the spiritual leader of our small family unit, we began a peaceful time at this lovely church tucked quietly in West Knoxville. It was comfortable to be a member of the congregation, but I don't remember the church community, or religion being a cornerstone of our family life. We didn't talk about our faith, nor was it something either parent pushed on the kids. In fact, I don't believe we had a very good attendance record. We weren't as bad as the twice-a-year crowd (Christmas and Easter), but we missed more Sundays than we made. Dad didn't share his thoughts about God or the Bible. He always struck me as silent and disengaged. Later in life, that changed, and he became more committed to his faith, but as I remember it, mom was the driver of Christian beliefs growing up.

Despite her position as household moral leader, mom didn't frequently project her spirituality verbally. As such, I never thought of mom as religious, but she believed, had faith, and adhered to Jesus' teachings. I think mom would've described herself as more spiritual than religious. She didn't like the drama or expectations that can come with church life.

Considering that I was raised outside the structure of enforced religion, I share the feelings my mom had. I believe, and I have faith, but I just don't need or want someone to remind me of that obligation, nor to work so hard to ensure I live up to their standards. Mom never would've said it that way, but were she here today, she would smile at me and nod in agreement.

Isolation is an easy way to worship privately, and that's all well and good, but what happens when faced with a tragedy and you're not embedded in a church support system? How did mom react? Was she drawn closer to God or was she angry? I often have wondered what role her Christian beliefs played in the battle she fought. I don't recall there being an enhanced emphasis on God or religion. The subject didn't suddenly become a topic that was always front and center. Thus, I don't think mom became more devout when she got cancer.

I also don't believe she became angry at God. It would be easy to do, and many believers develop insurmountable doubts about their faith. As humans, we want to blame something or someone, to feel anger and express that anger. It would be natural to question the higher power and ask, "Why did you let this happen to me?"

The Bible says in Hebrews, Chapter 11, Verse 1: "Now faith is the assurance of things hoped for, the evidence of things not seen." It's a statement espousing complete trust and confidence. It's comforting, but is it sustainable? How can someone avoid inevitable doubts when you're stricken? Many can't; thus, their commitment to believe faithfully is lowered. For others, questioning one's faith can reaffirm commitment, requiring that you consider your doubts boldly, allow your thoughts to wander outside of your previous biases, aggressively seek answers, then patiently acknowledge that faith doesn't always offer answers––it only offers hope, and the need to accept that truth as being good enough.

Mom prayed for hope and asked for strength to do what she didn't think she could do. I personally don't think praying could've given her a newfound ability, nor do I believe she thought that either. She prayed so she would have something to believe in, to have confidence in, to soothe her troubled soul. I have faith that praying gave her hope.

### *April 26, 1994*

*Today has been a very restful day. I have spent a lot of time in my corner, and my hip feels much better tonight. It makes me wonder what is going to happen to me when I return to work. It seems like any activity causes pain to increase. <u>What is going to happen to me?</u>*

*Dear Lord, please help me. It seems I am going to have to make a big decision if I return to work and the pain returns. I feel so much better since I have been off. Please guide me. Should I just go back and try, or should I just force myself to try and ignore the pain? Life is short, and I want so much to spend time with my husband, children, mother, and the rest of my family. Please guide me. Dear God, thank you for the beautiful day. The flowers are so beautiful, it makes my days much easier. Thank you for Ray and mom and my wonderful boys. Thank you also for all of my friends and our church family. Thank you so much for mother's return to good health and please help Ray recover completely. Amen.*

Being grateful when times are desperate isn't an easy thing to do. It's much easier to fall prey to the negative drain of emotions and allow your thoughts to compound negatively, to develop a perspective so that only doom and gloom hang over you. At this point, mom's outlook isn't good, and the road she's beginning to travel is full of more bumps than I think she knew. And yet, her gratitude prayer above indicated her willingness to be grateful for what was in her life. It feels good reading this, and I suspect she felt better after she wrote it.

For some people, being grateful is a natural trait, a tendency to view things in a positive light and consider all opportunities as gifts. This isn't the same thing as being an optimist, who views the world as a glass that's always half full. A grateful person understands that sometimes things aren't good, yet finds a way to appreciate the good around them and channel their gratitude to build strength and face challenges.

A few years ago, I was fortunate to have dinner with Nando Parrado, author of *Miracle in the Andes*. Nando was one of 16 survivors of the 1972 plane crash in the Andes Mountains that killed 29 people. Nando was a member of the Old Christians Club rugby team that was flying to Chile for a match. He was 22 at the time of the crash. After 72 days stranded at 11,712 feet in the snow-covered Andes, Nando and Roberto Canessa decided to walk off the mountain to seek help. After 10 days traversing steep peaks and deep snow, they were rescued.

It's an amazing story that has been retold for decades as an example of perseverance and the power of the human spirit. As I listened to Nando describe his time on the mountain and the dangerous trek to safety, I was on the edge of my seat. It was riveting and a story I'll never forget, but it wasn't his retelling of the epic tale that changed my life. It was Nando's conclusion of what it all meant.

He said the person he was before the crash died on the mountain. To him, that person was gone––but he viewed it as a gift: "Most people assess their life in their final days and wish they could alter things or have more time to do things. I died on the mountain at age 22, and then embarked on living out the rest of my life. I have never worried about what will happen or could happen. I can, and have, handled everything. I have remained grateful for every day, every breath, every moment I have experienced, good and bad."

Nando has lived a full life, having built one of the most successful business empires in South America and becoming a guiding light for people worldwide. He accomplished this because of how he lived, and also because he found gratitude at the beginning of his new-found life, propelling him to a joyous existence.

When mom was going through her journey and wrote

this entry, I hadn't yet understood the power of gratitude. I wish I had. I think I would've practiced more gratitude and joy with every small moment I had with her. All too often, I wanted to recapture what our life was like before the disease, but that was undoable. I should've relished each chance to be grateful. Mom was alive, and yes, her life wasn't easy, but she had so much to offer. I wish I'd asked her about her life, taken moments to listen to her stories, enjoyed the warmth of her smile and the joy I felt when we talked––and asked her whether she had secret recipes. I was moving too fast when I should've been slowing down.

Today, I'm committed to infusing my body with gratitude. I know that it isn't always easy to value everything that happens in life, and I know that those around me–– and me someday––will be facing a situation similar to mom's. When it happens, I'll reread mom's beautiful gratitude prayer and remember that we're given a reason to feel blessed every day. It's our job to recognize and embrace it.

### April 27, 1994

*I've done a little bit of everything today. Prepared pictures to mail, solved some billing problems (medical bills) for mom, and a bill sent to Randy, and cleaned out the closets for Ray and I. Pretty exciting, huh? It seems that the least amount of activity starts my hip hurting again. I don't think Ray understands. Ray has always thought that there was a reason for everything that happens.*

*Everything that happens has to be someone's fault. I don't think he understands that I feel like I have no control of this situation.*

*Dear God, please help me try very hard and beat this disease. Maybe some of this is my fault. Maybe I don't try hard enough. Please help Ray and I both better understand each other and depend on you for our answers.*

Mom and dad didn't have a lot of arguments. Marriage isn't easy, but they were a good role model for unconditional love and support. I knew they cared for each other, and I never doubted their shared commitment to love, honor, and cherish each other. Neither asked for this, but almost 30 years into their marriage, they faced the realities of the marriage covenant's line "in sickness and in health."

Up until now, mom hadn't expressed frustration with how dad was handling her cancer's return. There was no indication that tension was building––but it was.

It is true that dad tended to seek a cause for everything that happened. I have no doubt that at times, he made her feel like she should've done more. He knew that blaming her was unfair, and he wouldn't have done it intentionally. Whatever he said was likely an emotional moment. In marriage, we all have them. How many times have I said to myself, "Don't say that," then immediately said that? Too many.

Dad's outward communication was masking a deeper feeling: He was beginning to struggle. Mom was trying to process that she was going to die, sooner rather than later, but dad was too. His life partner was fading. All their dreams and his vision of growing old together were gone. He was facing a new reality, and it was weighing on him.

The role of primary caregiver for a spouse is profoundly difficult. You're forced to maintain your own life as you knew it––to work, pay bills, and keep the house functioning––but you're also tasked with providing care for someone who has different needs than they had before. You're now faced with doing things you aren't experienced at, advocating for your loved one, and staying strong and at the ready. It's exhausting and often causes the caregiver to lose their identity.

Dad was very hesitant to talk about his feelings openly, but when he did, it was obvious that he was scared. He never expressly said to me that he accepted mom was dying, but he was beginning to internalize that life would never be the same.

My sense is that we failed to provide dad with the means to support his mental health. I don't remember even thinking about this, and that was a mistake. I know he became lonely. A house that once felt like a daily festival now was dark, quiet, and––frankly––depressing. I can't imagine a bigger change for dad. It makes me sad just thinking about it.

There's something overwhelming about the notion of caring for someone while also grieving for them and for yourself. Dad wasn't dying, but his best friend was. Dad was about to turn 50, and his future was uncertain.

He didn't know what would happen to mom and what he was going to do, and he didn't have anyone he was willing to talk to. He became more and more isolated.

### *April 30, 1994*

*Well, the past two days have been a mixture of ups and downs. Thursday, I decided to ride with Ray to Sevier County. It was good to be out in the beautiful sunshine. We had a lovely lunch. We rented four movies and watched one of them Thursday night.*

*The anti-inflammatory drug is really starting to bother me. I wake up during the night with acid backing up in my mouth. I got an appointment with Dr. Barnett. I always feel better after seeing him even though he is very blunt and honest with me. He changed my medications and talked with me about my cancer. He said the only difference between me and him was that I knew what was going to kill me and at this time he didn't. He said none of us were guaranteed a certain life span. I told him that death wasn't what I was worried about. I was worried about what I would have to go through before I died. He also told me that if they watched me real close and could keep me alive for two or three years more, he thought there would be a cure for breast cancer. He assured me they would not let me suffer.*

*Dear God, thank you for Dr. Barnett and all of the other doctors who gave me such good care.*

*Please help me regain enthusiasm for life. Right now, I seem to have lost my zest and excitement for life. Help me deal with this cancer and continue to live. Sometimes giving up seems easier than going on. Please help me set an example for my family as well as others. Don't let me drag my family into the despair I now feel. Please help other people who are dealing with illnesses. Please show me the way. Amen.*

I know I shouldn't be harboring these thoughts, and that I'm an ass for feeling this way, but this diary entry frustrated me. There's a matter-of-fact acceptance of her imminent death, and I admire her for that. She says she isn't despondent over the outcome, and that makes sense, as denying your circumstances isn't helpful. However, it's her focus that bothers me.

Cancer is lonely. Despite the countless people who are involved in treating you, caring for you, or emotionally connected through friendship or family ties, cancer patients tend to live inside their heads, consumed with private thoughts and their own personal demons. It's a very challenging existence, and I understand that. At least I think I do. What I struggle with is mom's exclusive obsession with what she's going to have to go through and how her cancer is affecting her family. I distinctly remember these two thoughts dominating mom. No longer did she have a spark for the future or any hopeful optimism. She was stuck in this roundabout without an exit lane. Sadly, if that's all you're thinking about, you're destined to have a miserable time, and mom was miserable. There's no hint that she's trying to find meaning in her remaining days, no reflection on the impact she's had, no thoughts about how she wants to go out, and no mention of trying to do something impactful in her final days.

I'm not suggesting that she was going to do something to change the world or alter the course of history. However, I am suggesting that she could've spent her days creating memories and imparting her life wisdom and perspective to others. What fun we would've had spending time memorializing her recipes and reminiscing about the times she prepared them for the throngs of guests in our home.

I understand that I'm being too judgmental, assuming that she should've been able to live her life with more active intent, but honestly, my own personal, bold expectations may not work when I'm in her shoes. It's frightening to consider. I cannot imagine spending all my time knowing that I was dying, worrying about what it was going to be like, and afraid I was harming those I love. It sounds like a horrible existence.

Looking back and remembering how I felt when this was happening, I'm reminded how difficult it was to be around mom. I'm not saying I wasn't sad—I was 27 years old and I was devastated, I wanted something out of our remaining days together, and mom wasn't thinking that way.

Maybe I should've figured out how to ignore what was happening and make the best of it, but I wasn't raised that way. Mom raised me to charge ahead, to believe in something and go for it. Mom wasn't going to beat cancer, and her time was short, but I felt like she was wasting it. I didn't understand what she was trying to do. She was fighting the disease and putting herself through horrible treatments, but her mind was trapped, and she wasn't allowing her thoughts to go beyond her two fears.

I promised myself that I'd honor mom when I read her diary. The entry above from April 30, 1994, hasn't changed my intent, nor my view of mom. I'm not disparaging her feelings, nor her reaction to her situation. I'm expressing a frustration that I carried for years. Mom spent her last years fixated on her cancer treatment and how it impacted those she loved, a focus that brought her no joy, peace, meaning, or happiness. She had fallen into a well she couldn't climb out of it.

I'll always believe I should've found a way to alter her mindset, but that's likely wishful thinking. I honestly don't know what I could've done to alleviate her fixations, as she was stubborn. Maybe it wasn't going to happen. It makes me sick to my stomach to relive it.

We're all going to die. Some of us will do it slowly and will have the opportunity to shape those last few horrible months. I pray that if I'm in that situation, I'll turn sadness and suffering into a peaceful journey. I'm sad mom didn't do that. I'm sad for her and all of us who were around her.

### May 1, 1994

*Today, Ray and I decided we were going to rest all*

*day to get ready for the next week. It turned out to be so boring and depressing. I discovered today that I was depressing my mom when I told her everything. Dr. Barnett said he has been so happy with her attitude and great new outlook on life, and now I've ruined it. I don't think I really worry about dying, but I am tired of hurting all the time. This depresses me because I can't do anything, but I am going to have to be more positive in my actions for my family's sake.*

*Dear God, please help me be strong and handle the pain better. I do not want to drag my family down, and that is what I am doing. Please help me. Help my mother get through this period and return to her happy self. Please be with me tomorrow as I return to work. Thank you for my wonderful job and the great people I work with. Amen.*

My previous reaction to mom's entry was too harsh. It reflects my lingering frustration and anger at the disease and what happened to mom. Although I don't know for sure, but based on her prior diary entries and my memory of the time, I believe mom was clinically depressed. I understand that depression isn't a feeling, it's a clinical condition that alters your mood, your daily routine, and your physical and emotional state. It also isn't widely understood. Most lay people think when someone says they're depressed, it's no more than a passing feeling that the afflicted can turn off and get back to living a normal life. It's not that simple. Research has shown that major depression is often brought on by biological, psychological, or social stress. It's a response to a negative event, or set of events, that alters the brain's neuro-circuitry and causes it to misfire.

The body is an impressive creation. In normal circumstances—i.e., in vibrant, healthy individuals—it operates as a complex set of systems with aligned functions. However, when things go wrong, the body has a way of creating a negative compounding effect. It isn't enough that a person is experiencing trauma. Stress leads the body to react, and the reaction is usually counterproductive. Instead of your body finding a way to rally, it stumbles. One problem can, and often does, lead to another. The interconnectivity is amazing.

Mom was demonstrating the signs of clinical depression. Her sleep was affected, her mood was altered, despair dominated her mind, and her self-esteem was diminished. She was struggling, and the weight of all she carried was beginning to overwhelm her.

I always suspected that mom and mamaw both struggled with depression. Even before cancer, I recall times when I heard them talk about Prozac. My sense is that they were susceptible to depression prior to mom's cancer. Her cancer diagnosis only made it worse, for both.

My need to solve things makes the subject of depression frustrating. Despite my aforementioned disappointment with how mom's spirit degenerated, I frankly don't know how a person in mom's condition, who has shown tendencies toward bouts of depression, could've navigated this without falling into a dark place. I also don't think there's much of anything well-intentioned loved ones can do to change the situation materially. Accepting it as a wiring problem in the brain, nothing short of medication and a good physician will make a difference.

Mom frequently references her conversations with Dr. Barnett about her depression in the diary, indicating how these conversations boosted her mood. However, that wasn't enough. I don't know whether she was on medication for depression during this period, but I do know that she used Xanax for anxiety. Unlike best-of-class anti-depressants, which try to address the underlying cause of neurotransmitters' failure to operate correctly, Xanax calms anxiety. It's a Band-Aid, not a solution. It's prescribed to be taken as needed. That broad direction leaves it to the patient to decide when they need it.

Sadly, there's a bigger problem than the difficulty with one-on-one treatment options. Society doesn't want to address mental illness. It's not a subject that makes people feel warm. In fact, it usually makes people uncomfortable. As such, treatments for and research on mental illness are woefully lacking. Frankly, I don't think I've ever known of any black-tie charity event to raise money for clinical depression.

The stigmatization and lack of conversation about depression make it a condition that the afflicted and their families rarely talk about. I know that in all the time mom was sick, the subject of her depression never came up, yet it played such a major role in her life. Her inability to climb out of her mental condition led to a substantially altered lifestyle, reduced human interactions, a loss of spirit, and a much greater dependence on addictive meds.

Certainly, the cancer treatments impacted her life and reduced her strength. However, the vicious cycle of mental anguish and symptoms of major depression played an outsized role in mom's final years.

I only can hope that the medical community has learned to better communicate with patients and their families about clinical depression's potential to present itself, treatment options, the risk of drug abuse, and the impact it can have on terminal patients. Roughly 3 million people in the US are newly diagnosed each year with major depression. The human brain is designed brilliantly, yet things can go wrong. As a society, as healthcare professionals, and as humans, we need to be better at addressing mental health. The problem isn't going to go away.

### May 6, 1994

*Well, the past few days have been traumatic. I have been to three different doctors, and right now, it appears that I have a tumor in the pubic bone. Tomorrow, another MRI. Thursday, a decision on what to do. It appears the cancer is aggressive, and if we don't treat it the same way, it is going to spread all over. We'll know Thursday where we stand. We have all cried, and I am trying to prepare myself mentally and physically for chemo.*

*Please, dear God, help us all accept your will with this cancer. I know you can heal me or at least give me some time. This is hard on my family*

*and friends. Please help them deal with it too. Be*
*with us when we try to make the right decision*
*for treatment. The next six days are going to seem*
*very long, and we are going to be anxious. I pray*
*that you teach me patience. Amen.*

Metastatic breast cancer is referred to as stage IV. Most commonly, it presents itself as new tumors in the bones, lungs, liver, or brain. The new tumors are a result of breast cancer cells spreading from the original cancer site in the breast either through the bloodstream or the lymphatic system. As a result, it's not uncommon today for a patient to have their lymph nodes removed. Mom initially had her nodes tested, but they weren't removed.

A metastasized tumor found in a bone comprises cells from the original breast cancer that have relocated. Thus, the same treatment that was used for earlier stages of breast cancer typically is used to treat the discovered tumor. The fact that mom developed bone tumors——first in her hip, then in her pelvic bone——isn't unusual. These bones commonly are affected when breast cancer metastasizes. It's also widely accepted that her complaints about joint and bone pain are an indicator of potential cancer development in the bones.

Cruelly, breast cancer cells can take months or years to find a new home and become stage IV cancer. The intervening period creates a constant cloud of doubt in the patient's mind. The fear of not knowing and wondering whether cells from your original cancer are lying in wait somewhere in your body and have yet to strike is daunting.

Sadly, when the big fear is realized, prospects for the future are reduced. In 1994, when mom faced the reality of another bone tumor, her future was bleak.

She mentions that the cancer was aggressive. I honestly don't know how the doctors knew that or could say that. Today, oncologists can type genetic markers and have a much better understanding of what the cells are likely to do. When the doctors told her this, they were doing it based on limited data and a view of the pace of cell growth that they could see. Nothing more.

It had been roughly 16 months between her first diagnosis of breast cancer and when she learned of the tumor in her hip. Now five months later, another tumor has been found. In the months since her initial breast surgery, she's struggled to find her footing. The stress of what could happen, her growing dependency on medications, her mental challenges with depression, and her generally poor health resulted in the post-diagnosis period being a struggle. Some people rally quickly after they have surgery and begin to thrive again. Mom didn't thrive and was barely able to survive.

I don't know what it means to measure mom's experience vs. those of others. It isn't fair, nor is it helpful. It was what it was. From the moment mom woke up in the hospital and asked me what happened during the initial surgery, until she was told the cancer was spreading and was aggressive, mom wasn't the same person. To be fair, those around her weren't the same either. Mom always had been a rock for me and those in her life. Seeing her diminished altered us. I know it did me.

It's useless to play "what if." It only leads to frustration and regrets. However, there's a takeaway for me. You just never know. Every day is a blessing, whatever happens. With that mindset, it's incumbent on us all to value each day and try and get the most out of your time here. I think mom thought the time immediately after her cancer was detected would be the hardest stage and that it would get better. What she didn't know was that the months after her surgery and before the bone tumors would be the best moments she had left in her life. It wasn't going to get better; it was going to get a lot worse.

### *May 11, 1994*

*Doubt! That has been the word facing me these past few days. After all the signs that the cancer was back, the MRI I had Saturday showed nothing, according to the radiologist at Parkwest. Because we doubted that the test was correct, Dr. Arwood had the films brought to TCSC. The experts in reading MRIs found two spots of cancer in my hip and pelvic area. You talk about my confidence being shattered. I WAS SHATTERED. Now I doubt all the tests in the past. I wonder if my pelvic cancer found in December would've been found in September if the X-rays had been read by experts.*

*Dear God, thank you for leading us to Dr. Arwood for help. He insisted on going one step further. I have been full of doubt about my tests from the beginning. For the first time, I have faith in one of my cancer doctors. And of course, faith is*

*very important. Thank you very much for granting*
*me this peace of mind. This past week has been very*
*trying, and I thank you for helping us get through*
*this. Please help my family. Amen.*

The roller coaster continues. I don't know how anyone can function normally with wild swings of information and variables constantly pushing you around. It isn't fair. I know life's not fair, and having cancer damn sure isn't fair, but this seems cruel.

Mom's lack of confidence in her treatment and past tests is justified, but it masked the sad truth: Mom's cancer was spreading, and there was no doubt as to her disease's trajectory.

It's precisely at a moment like this when mom, or any other patient, would wonder whether things would've been different had her doctors done a better job. What if they'd removed her lymph nodes? Did they give her the optimal amount of radiation or chemo? More importantly, what if the mammography she had nine months before her diagnosis had detected cancer? All these possibilities might have altered her outcome. However, finding that the cancer had spread into her bones earlier wouldn't have mattered. Once it metastasized, the prognosis was the same. In my view, replaying prior events doesn't help.

However, it's human nature. No matter how hard we try to avoid dwelling on moments in our life that we'd like to change, people generally still allow themselves to look backward. It often begins as a nod to "I wish that hadn't happened." Next comes regret. It can be in the form of a common question, such as, "What do you regret in your life?" or "What would you have done differently?"

These thoughts aren't necessarily bad. Reflecting on your past can be helpful if you're learning from something you did or that happened. Best case scenario: Maybe it'll help you avoid a similar mistake in the future. This process is how humans learn. It's essentially a form of reinforcement learning. Remember: You only touch a hot stove once before you recognize that doing it again is a bad idea.

Beyond regret, the next level of revisionism is bitterness. When your past becomes something that enters your consciousness and causes you to feel anger or hate toward someone or something, it can be debilitating. A good friend of mine once told me, "Bitterness is like you drinking poison and hoping the person you're mad at dies."

It's easy to chronicle how looking in the rearview mirror can be counterproductive. It's hard in real life to avoid falling into the trap. Letting go is inherently not how most people function. I know because I've struggled to accept my past and forgive those whom I perceive have done me wrong.

I've found that the only way to move beyond my tendency to focus on past mistakes is to practice forgiveness of others and myself. Studies show that people who consistently forgive are happier and more at peace. I believe in the power of forgiveness. I also know it's hard as hell.

My reaction to mom's diary entry is different today than if I had read this when I was in my early 30s. Maybe

I'm making progress. I hope so. I do know that I can credit mom and her loving soul for my ability to become a more forgiving person. Before mom was sick, I was aware of and admired her ability to find something positive in people. She wasn't perfect, but she wanted to accept whatever happened and to practice forgiveness.

The events surrounding her MRI shattered mom's confidence, and that makes sense. Her reaction is what you would expect. However, it didn't linger. I don't recall mom obsessing over what did or didn't happen, i.e., she didn't become bitter. Despite her tragic path, she didn't lose this aspect of her being. She remained the loving, accepting soul who gave the gift of forgiveness to all who loved her.

# CHAPTER 8

### May 15, 1994

*Well, I am going to Duke. After the last set of circumstances (the misreading of the films), Dr. Kerns called Duke, and they agreed to take me on as a patient. All this week, I must have tests at Parkwest and bone marrow drawn by Dr. Kerns. I will find out tomorrow when I will go to Duke.*

*This weekend has been really good. Mike and Ashley came up Friday night, then Rick, Rebecca, and Brittany came up Saturday. I really had a good night with my children. I was able to block most of the worry out of my mind for at least a couple days. Today, Ray and I went to see Tennessee play baseball. It was really good to get out among people.*

*But tomorrow, reality sets in again when I go to the hospital and Dr. Kerns' office for my prep for some of my tests. This is not going to be an easy week.*

*Mom looks very sad, and I am very worried about her. She has been so happy until now. This cancer ruins everybody's life.*

*Mike is also concerned. I could tell by the way he treated me this weekend that he is very concerned.*

*Dear God, please help us all get through this. I pray for healing, but if that is not your will, I pray you help my family accept this and get on with their lives. I also pray that you will not let me suffer. Sometimes I feel like I have been sick for a very long time, and I am very tired. Thank you for my beautiful family and the fact that they are such good people. Please be with Mike as he works so hard for his family. Also be with Tiff and Rick and Rebecca as they work to provide for their families and still be good parents. Please forgive Ray and I for being so lax in our church attendance. You know the reasons. Some of them are good, some not. Please forgive me for my sins. Amen.*

I WAS CONCERNED. MOM LOOKED BAD. Her skin color was off, her smile seemed forced, and her engaging personality was missing. The last two years had aged her, and she seemed like she was fading. I hadn't seen her in a few months, and I was taken aback when I walked into the house. I know she saw my reaction. I'm disappointed that I showed my feelings so easily. She didn't need to see me look at her that way.

Dad also was troubled. He was quiet and disconnected. Time wasn't treating him well, and I could see he needed a break. We talked a bit, and for the first time, he shared his concerns, albeit reluctantly. He didn't know what to do. He wanted mom to fight and beat the cancer, but he also saw how her battle was taking a massive toll on her. He said he was lost—torn between providing emotional support for her fight and wondering whether it's all worth it. It was an impossible place for him to be, and I immediately felt sorry for him.

Being the oldest son in my family and the oldest cousin from mamaw's offspring, I always felt a responsibility. Maybe it was more like pressure. I don't really know, but I typically found myself acting older than my age. As a result, I tended to be arrogant. It was silly to be so confident and self-assured, but for whatever reason, I wore my ego for all to see. I didn't realize how I came across until later in life. I'm privately embarrassed when I remember some of my less-than-impressive moments. Sadly, my attitude caused problems in various relationships within my extended family and my cohort group. I didn't mean to be cocky, but I was.

After realizing my own perception of my role, and considering the historically close relationship I had with mom, I decided I needed to have a private conversation with her. As I write this, it sounds like such a self-important notion, and it probably was. My intentions were good, as I was trying to help mom and dad.

Sitting on the front porch, in our old rocking chairs, a

place that still holds countless memories of deep, loving, thoughtful conversations, I slowly began to talk to mom about what was happening.

Eventually, I got to the primary point and asked her, "Do you want to fight this cancer?"

She paused for a few seconds and slowly said, "Yes."

"Why?" I asked.

"I have one reason: I want to live long enough for the grandkids to remember me. That's it for me."

She looked at me, and tears filled her eyes. Her face was pained as she allowed a small smile to break through. She looked so lonely and afraid. It was one of the saddest moments of my life and a memory I'll never shake.

I leaned forward to get out of my chair and go hug mom, but she motioned with her hand for me to sit back down. She had something more she wanted to say.

"Please help me do this," She said. "It's the most important thing I have left."

I promised her I'd do everything I could to support her desire to live long enough to have a connection with the grandkids.

We didn't say anything else for a long time, just slowly rocked to the rhythms of a peaceful Southern evening. I don't know how long we sat quietly thinking about what was just said, our shared life, our love for each other, and our friendship. I don't know, and I don't care. I'll never forget the moment's complexity.

On one hand, we were connecting like we always had; our bond was powerfully deep, and we both knew it. On the other hand, this damned cancer had pushed us apart.

I couldn't describe it then, and I struggle now. It was as though the basis for how we talked had shifted. Mom always gave me a sense of control, even when it wasn't real. Talking to her reinforced in me that anything was possible. Cancer destroyed the idea of control. Mom didn't control anything, and I didn't control anything, so chatting didn't give us the comfort that we could make anything possible. It was a damaging blow to the foundation of how we communicated.

There was more. After mom's initial treatment, she began to close me off. It was subtle, but real. She seemed guarded when we talked. I wonder how much of this was her and how much of it was me.

I changed too. For the first time in my life, I realized that something bad was about to happen to someone I loved, and I was powerless.

Like most relationships, a few hiccups between a parent and child don't make much of an impact. However, a prolonged shift in the dynamics of how two people interact begins to become the new norm. For mom and me, our new norm was a silent, fearful detachment.

However, on that one night in the spring of 1994, we were able to spend time together and talk candidly. I feel blessed that our intimate conversation on the front porch was a positive experience. For a brief moment, there remained some semblance of who we were.

Feeling the need to move ahead, we simultaneously stood up and hugged each other with heartfelt sincerity. It also felt like a hug of resignation. It was both beautiful and sad.

I don't think that specific chat brought us closer, or even closed the gap that had formed in our relationship. However, it did give me perspective. Mom clearly stated her purpose for fighting, and I hoped that it would carry her through what was coming.

I also immediately recognized what mom was saying. Ashley and Brittany were about 2 years old. Thomas was three months away from being born. Was she really saying that she wanted to live another six years? Was that possible? The odds were against her. For mom to live to achieve her goal, she was going to need luck, endure brutal treatments, and maybe get some divine intervention.

On the drive home, I thought about what mom had said, what dad was feeling, the hard truth about her situation, and her desire to endure for something meaningful. I was proud of mom, but also terrified. I didn't believe she could pull it off, but I was absolutely committed to doing my part.

### May 22, 1994

*Well, this past week has been something. I started off the week being sick, then the rest of the week I spent having tests at the hospital and doctor's office. Two more tests this week, then we are going to Duke. The tests have been rough, but I think things are going to get worse before they get better. It is really strange how I feel. I really don't know how I feel. The only thing I know is I'm very tired. Very tired. If it weren't for my family, I would just give up and not have anything done. I'm tired.*

*Dear God, please give me the strength to go on. I do want to see my grandchildren grow up, and I want to watch my children succeed in life. Amen.*

### May 23, 1994

*I feel very scared tonight. I had a bone scan today, and the time is getting closer and closer to finding out something definitive about my situation. I'm also afraid of the biopsy Wednesday. Sometimes I feel like I'm not even in my body. It seems I go through the motions of living. I get up when I'm supposed to get up. I eat when I'm supposed to eat. I say all the right things to people. People think I am strong, but I doubt that I am. Outside I'm strong. On the inside, I'm scared. Cancer is controlling my whole being. There are very few times that cancer is not on my mind. I think finding out something more definitive will help. I think I can stand the treatment if I know it is going to help me feel better in the long run and buy me some time. But I hate <u>waiting.</u> I guess one of my favorite times of the day is when I can go to bed. My bedroom and my bed are a haven for me. I also know that when I can't stand it any longer, I can take my sleeping pill and go to sleep. I sometimes do that so I don't have to feel pain. I try to stay busy, but I am limited to what I can do. I hate waiting.*

Prior to reading this entry, It never occurred to me that one of mom's big frustrations was her loss of control.

Obviously, she was never in control of the course of her disease, nor the outcome, but what I failed to appreciate and that was far more insidious was the negative impact that losing her decision-making ability had on her. Mom describes doing everything exactly as she's supposed to without variation. I didn't notice that happening to her, and I doubt anyone else did either. But I get her sentiment. In an effort to help mom, we all began to structure her life for her. As is often the case, good intentions lead to unintended consequences.

I'm sure this was annoying. In fact, it was probably maddening. At the very moment she's vulnerable to an outside attack, she loses her freedom. Obviously, that doesn't work, as we all want to feel as though we have a say in how we exist.

Learning that mom felt this way and her comments about bedtime also provide me with new insight. Mom talks about her happiness when she's in her bed, when it's time to end the day. Importantly, she mentions her habit of taking "my sleeping pill."

It feels like this was important to her because it represented a small action she could control. I think she concluded that management of her medications was her domain and that she owned it. I never considered that her growing consumption of drugs was more than just about pain or forgetting reality, but it was. It seems clear that it was a private demonstration that she was in control. Because mom was free to select the time, and frankly the amount she took, she possessed a powerful mechanism to exert some control.

I recognize that I'm not qualified to determine the cause of mom's growing dependency. Nevertheless, it makes sense that she gained comfort from knowing she could alter a small part of her day. From her perspective, she was forced to do what everyone else said she must do. However, at the end of the day, she could do what she wanted, and it brought her peace.

Mom's growing frustration with being managed and her need to find a way to be in charge underscored the importance of thinking through how you interact with a patient who's facing a terrible future. From the day we found out she had cancer, we treated mom differently. She was used to managing the house and being the ringmaster. Once she got sick, we assumed she needed us to care for her, all the time. That wasn't true. She needed a semblance of her previous life. It needed to be her call as to how much she wanted to do, and how she wanted to do it.

Don't get me wrong—I don't believe for a minute that if mom had felt more in control, she wouldn't have struggled with pain meds. I think she still would have, but maybe she would've had a different mindset. Maybe that outlet wouldn't have reinforced her need for control.

As in the case with almost everything, I accept that we don't get a do-over. That's not my purpose in reflecting on what happened. Rather, I seek to better understand mom and who she was during her cancer battle, and it's working. Prior to the cancer, my connection with mom was natural and easy. I lost that when she got sick, and two decades later, I still feel a void. However, the gap is closing.

## May 26, 1994

*Well, I didn't write last night because I was out of it. Yesterday, Dr. Williams did a bone biopsy to confirm the cancer in my pelvis. He was such a kind and caring doctor. He was very patient and careful, and was sure to give me pain medication as I needed it. I had a lot of confidence in him, and that is something I have not had in some of my doctors recently.*

*I got the results from the biopsy done yesterday, and it was malignant. We all knew that it was just a matter of getting a good biopsy. I know it is not good news to find out that a biopsy is positive, but in this case, it was just confirmation. Dr. Williams hit the spot just right. So, finally, everything seems to be falling into place. I have been in pain for two years, and I am ready to do something to try to put the cancer in remission and get some relief from this pain.*

Bone cancer is known to be the most painful form of cancer. The pain is chronic and can be debilitating. There's no escaping it––bone cancer is miserable.

It is obvious that mom needed better advocacy from her family, and I blame myself for that. As she's described several times, she was in pain for a long time. The pain she described is a classic, early indicator of bone cancer, and tumors in bones are the most likely location for breast cancer to spread. In mom's case, it had been more than a year since she began to complain about pain in her hip, and the sense of urgency from her doctors was lacking.

At a minimum, an advocate could've pushed for quicker action. If there had been a stronger sense of urgency, it would've helped mom's attitude and provided momentum. Mom would've benefitted from this, as it was in her nature to feel optimistic. Reading her diary describe her countless hours of treatment and interactions with the medical community, it feels like everyone was resigned to what was going to happen. I get that. Working with oncology patients must be a very draining experience. We're blessed that caregivers are willing to provide care to patients who are as sick as mom, and yet, it's hard for a patient to have hope when you spend all your time waiting and wondering what's next. Rather than gain a hopeful mindset, it sounds like the cancer center is where hope goes to die.

I didn't know at the time what the doctors viewed as the gold standard treatment for stage IV breast cancer in the bones, but today it's believed that chemo makes little impact on managing the cancer. Radiation is used to help with pain management, but it doesn't typically offer long-term remission. There aren't many good choices. The time a patient has left has more to do with how aggressive the cancer is growing.

Mom then headed to Duke for treatment. I remember feeling a sense of relief. World-class teaching hospitals can provide better care, and often they will try alternative strategies. It's a research environment, and they're seeking new answers. It isn't that their patients are guinea pigs.

They're typically extremely sick and, in most cases, seeking something different or a miracle. Mom was certainly praying for both.

# CHAPTER 9

**June 6, 1994**

*A lot has happened in the past couple of weeks. The cancer was confirmed, and earlier this week, I came to Duke. I have been entered into the bone marrow program. I guess we were all surprised this past week when the doctors at Duke explained to us that I needed to be treated, and it needed to be done right away. Mother, Ray, and I were shocked at the urgency with which they looked at my case. We went home knowing something needed to be done, and soon.*

*Today, Mother and I came back to Durham. We have run into a slight problem. One of my scans shows a little shadow on my lung. Before we can start chemo, I must have some tests done to determine what is in my lung. If the biopsy is clean, then I will enter the hospital and start chemo Thursday.*

*Ray was very sad today when we left. I feel so sorry for him. It is very hard to stay behind by yourself and not know what is going on. Mom is a real trooper and will be here with me all the time she can for this chemo.*

*The few days between our first visit to Duke and now were very busy. Now I am lying in bed at the Brownstone Inn, and I'm scared about the test tomorrow—not just the biopsy, but the fact I could have lung cancer.*

THIS CONFIRMS MY MEMORY. Things started moving fast when mom went to Duke. They are built to handle extreme cases. When a patient was admitted into the cancer program, they were already in dire straits. Whatever treatment plan they tried wasn't working, and they were running out of time.

A teaching hospital like Duke is different. It's cutting edge, innovative, and pushing the envelope. Within the health system, attending physicians serve in the capacity of lead doctors and primary teaching faculty. Other physicians are in their fellowship programs and residents who have just begun their careers as doctors. It's a learning environment. Doctors are either principally teaching or learning. It fosters a dynamic, constant, high-paced setting.

Because the ecosystem is moving rapidly with new

teaching rotations, patients experience a different dynamic at a teaching hospital. They aren't treated by their "normal" local doctors, and unlike back home, they rarely build a long-term relationship with their attending physicians. It doesn't mean that the doctors aren't professional or pleasant; it just tends to be a very matter-of-fact existence. Honestly, that's OK and fitting. A world-class academic medical center reflects its reality: very sick patients seeking a better outcome, surrounded by some of the best doctors who have experience in a given specialty and a commitment to advancing their patients' care and medicine as a whole.

Duke oncologists' vast experience allowed them to understand that mom needed to act immediately. I don't know if they gave her verbal hope that she would get better, or if their rapid engagement was enough to give mom a sense of positive movement, but she had renewed optimism. I did too, but mine was different.

I held some deep-seated hope that Duke could change the direction of mom's cancer, but not much. They were one of the best-known cancer centers in the country, but being the best doesn't make you a miracle worker. I didn't believe a miracle was coming, but I hoped that Duke could give mom confidence in her clinical team, a clear understanding of what the treatment plan was, a roadmap for what she can expect, and removal of doubt. I believed that if mom could accept her future, whatever that was, then she could find herself before it was too late.

Privately, mom was in the same place. I'm sure she harbored more hope than I that a cure could be found, but more than anything, she needed to relinquish her medical future to people she trusted and find the strength to march ahead with comfort and peace. Since she was first diagnosed, mom hadn't been settled. A raging conflict consumed her, and her life had evolved into a gloomy, desperate vacuum. Duke was mom's last hope––for a cure, for comfort, and for her to regain who she was.

### June 7, 1994

*The lung biopsy was done yesterday, and now we are awaiting the results. Wait, wait, wait. The results of this test are so important to us all. If they come back negative, then I am on my way back to a possible recovery. If not, I have to find a new place to treat me, and that would be terrible. I have lots of people praying for me, and I know God will answer my prayers. It may not be in the way we think is right, but it will be the right answer.*

*Newsbreak: Lucy called, and my lungs are clear. No lung cancer. Thank you, dear God. Now I will enter the hospital Thursday to start chemo. I know it is going to be a tough road, but I will just pray for strength.*

*Dear God, thank you for hearing all the prayers that have been prayed for me. Thank you for my family and friends, and thank you for this opportunity to try and be healed. Please grant me lots of courage as I start this chemo. Be with my family—Ray, mom, Mike, Rick, and my sisters and all my other family who have stood beside me so strongly during this ordeal. I love them all so much. Amen.*

I admire mom and anyone else who faces a terrible path ahead with the temerity and toughness to march forward. She understood how bad this would be, accepted the long odds, and was still ready to proceed. Not everyone can do that. I remain hopeful that those who find the internal strength fight because of some sense of a greater purpose. It has to be present. How else could someone continue? Mom wanted to live for her grandchildren to know her. As a new papaw, I get the sentiment. If you're dying, the opportunity to have some modest influence on the next generation is special.

Outside of her stated objective, her willingness to struggle is still amazing. Most people can fight to live in the now. If an accident occurs, humans' instinct is to fight to live, but that's short-term. Mom had been fighting for two years, and it had been unrelenting. The burden of the disease, combined with the daily mental anguish she felt, created an environment in which she almost never had a break from her reality. It sounds exhausting.

And yet, there she was––taking the next step to delay the progression of her terminal disease. She had to know––and even embrace the expectation––that Duke wasn't going to play around with this. They were moving fast and were targeting her for the most extreme treatment in use within the bone marrow transplant program.

Mom wanted to live longer, and selfishly, I wanted mom back. It hurts me to acknowledge this, but I didn't think in terms of extra time or a cure, as that was too big an aspiration. I prayed that her pending treatments would give her a respite from cancer, such that she would be able to live like she was before, and that we'd be able to go back to our prior relationship.

This all happened so fast. Our life together had been stripped away abruptly, and I wanted it back. We hadn't had enough time. I was 25 when she was diagnosed. I'd been an adult for a little more than seven years, and mom was still in her 40s. There was so much more to do, to learn, to enjoy. Mom was still alive, but she wasn't the same. I wasn't the same. I didn't know it when she was diagnosed, but that event forever changed our time together. I began to grieve the loss of my mother after she got cancer, not when she died. For me, it made it worse. I know that's not fair. She wanted to live, and she went through so much to do that, but so much of who she was already had died.

It was unrealistic of me to believe that this new chapter of her fight could create an outcome that would reset her back to mom, but that was what I hoped for. I'm sure mom hoped for that too, but she had more immediate concerns. She wanted to live, to have her grandkids know her, and to imagine a life beyond hospital walls.

We were pinning a lot on Duke and their ability to perform miracles. Too much.

### June 9, 1994

*I'm in the hospital at Duke. I have been tested, X-rayed, and stuck since noon today. I have nurses,*

*doctors, and fellows who will be treating me. I*
*know there are many more to meet, but I am getting*
*tired tonight. I have been stuck with a catheter to*
*start the 5FU, but it hasn't come from the pharmacy*
*yet. I am scheduled to have surgery in the morning*
*to have my Hickman catheter put in. I am afraid*
*of what is going to happen to me, but others have*
*had all this done to them and survived. Maybe I*
*can too.*

*This is the first night of many bad nights to come.*

5FU is short for Flourouracil, a chemo drug used routinely for many types of cancer, including breast. Given alone, 5FU isn't that effective. The best results occur when it's administered in concert with other medications. Even though its individual use doesn't deliver great outcomes, it does provide its own unique, nasty side effects, including hair loss, sore mouth and throat, diarrhea, heart problems, difficulty breathing, and fatigue. Sounds awful, and it is.

I'm not sure how I'd feel today if I were sick and I knew that the treatment they were me offering wasn't likely to change the prognosis, but was almost certain to make me feel like hell. Doesn't sound like a good deal; however, there was more to it for mom. The drug is intended to slow cancer cells' growth. This blunting of cell growth was needed to prepare mom for her bone marrow transplant.

Mom's right. This initial activity was a small step down an arduous path. First, the warmup with 5FU, then a more toxic mix to attack the cancer cells, followed by initiation of the transplant protocol. I understand why she was scared and full of doubt.

You start to climb a big mountain by taking the first little step. Mom is doing that, and I'm proud of her, but I also feel cold. My mind takes me back to her hospital room—beeping sounds, unwelcoming lights, a shitty bed, constant interruptions, and nothing from home to make you feel settled. It's a frightening image to relive and brings out the saddest of emotions for me.

Why did this happen to mom? She didn't deserve this. Nobody does.

I felt then, and still do, that there are no words to say to a person in mom's situation. Nothing makes this better. I can't think of one thing I could've said to her that would've altered her emotional fragility. She knew I loved her. I told her that all the time. I guess if I could've told her, with absolute confidence, that everything was going to be OK, that would've given her more encouragement. But I couldn't do that, and she knew it. Any attempt to express certainty was hollow words. I didn't know what was going to happen.

I believe that mom's Christian faith was demonstrated during times like this. Mom often said, "If it's God's will, then it's his plan, and I can accept that." I think this was her way of handing her fate to a higher being, but also acknowledging that she had absolutely no control. She believed if she didn't have the deciding control, it's logical to defer your outcome to your faith.

Her approach, shared by many religious people, meant that she wasn't likely to blame God for whatever happened. She yielded her existence to a higher power and was willing to forge ahead peacefully knowing that the outcome would be what was supposed to happen. I respect that.

In my lifetime, I often have said, "It is what it is." I never thought of that as a nod to preordination, to a belief that all events already are defined. That concept makes no sense to me, nor do I think mom believed in that doctrine. However, acceptance that we, as humans, possess control over some of our actions, but not all outcomes, feels right to me. I think you can believe in both God and self-determination, and accept that we're not all-controlling.

Mom had to get to this place. There would be no way you could fight this disease if you believed you didn't have a role to play. It would be too overwhelming if you thought it was fruitless. Simultaneously, believing you had power to decide the outcome was crazy. All that mom or anyone else in this situation can do is their part to the best of their ability. Mom was embarking on a horrible journey. She was trying, and although the image of her lying in bed with tubes in her body makes me shiver, it also makes me fired up with pride how that tough, amazing woman asked for pain so she could live.

### June 9, 1994

*Well, I started my 5FU last night, and so far, so good. This morning, I had surgery to put in the Hickman catheter. The experience was not bad at all. I am having some pain, but the pain pills*

*do help. I am taking antibiotics since the surgery.*
*The nurse who is the contact nurse for home doctors*
*and Duke doctors met with me today. She upset me*
*because she questioned why I had taken Xanax,*
*Trazodone, antiinflammation, stomach medicine,*
*etc. She wanted to know if there was a special*
*reason why I had problems sleeping at night, and if*
*it had just been happening in the past few months*
*since I found out about metastatic breast cancer.*
*I told her this was not just a few months thing,*
*and that I'd been hurting since last summer and*
*had been trying to convince doctors that something*
*was wrong with me. I told her I had been upset*
*for almost two years.*

It isn't surprising that the medical team at Duke would explore mom's rationale for her prescription drug use. As the newest provider, they wanted to better understand mom's overall health and any variables that could impact her treatment. I also think that the inquiry reflects the teaching hospital environment's serious mindset. It can be blunt. Their focus is treating the disease.

However, mom's physicians in Knoxville had a history with her—in some instances, a friendship. The very nature of this close connectivity likely made it more difficult for physicians to be tough. It also was true in mom's case that she pestered them so often, they succumbed to her and willingly or unwillingly provided her with the drugs she wanted, when she wanted them.

The ease with which mom secured drugs like Xanax

was a problem. Certain drugs have a rebound effect, and that's particularly true for mind-altering drugs, both legal and illicit varieties. It becomes a vicious cycle: You take the drug, experience its impact, and when you don't have the medication in your body, you develop cravings that push you to recapture the feeling you had when it was impacting you. In fact, the bottom of the rebound usually creates a new baseline experience that's worse than what you felt at the outset. I don't definitively know whether Xanax typically follows this pattern, but it did for mom.

The more mom took Xanax, the more she felt anxiety when she wasn't taking it. Furthermore, things that hadn't bothered her before, impacted her. In short order, mom established a new "normal" in her life. That normal was having enough Xanax in her system until she felt nothing. When she teetered on the edge of feeling stress, her body told her she needed to stop the wave of anxiety. She needed to feel like "herself" again. She needed to be numb.

I don't know when mom started taking multiple Xanax pills simultaneously, but she did. Soon, it grew to two at once, then three. It isn't clear how many pills became the norm. I'm afraid to guess. It was a lot. Dad once told me she was getting prescriptions from multiple doctors for the same medication. This was before electronic medical records and data sharing between pharmacies and insurance companies. The only way her routine could've been broken is if the doctors, collectively, had communicated and coordinated on what she had access to.

I guess her family also could've stepped in and tried

to stop it, but that's damn hard. It would've had to fall on either dad or mamaw to step up, but it's not fair to expect that. They lived with mom and saw her suffer, and above all else, they wanted to take care of her. I know they knew this was a problem. I'm also sure they didn't have the strength to force the issue. Mom was sick and dying, and if they could make her feel better, they would support that.

Dad was more likely than mamaw to try, but to my knowledge, he didn't. I think mamaw also was managing stress with Xanax. In that regard, she was an enabler. It was an impossible situation. Duke would try, but they only could control what happened when she was in Durham. The Knoxville doctors had given up or chose to act oblivious. Dad couldn't, mamaw wouldn't, but what about me?

I felt guilty for not stepping in. I could've, should've. I didn't know what to do. I felt the tug between being a tough supporter and pushing her to change her habits against the never-ending awareness that I wasn't there. I didn't live through the day-to-day. How could I tell her how she should live when I almost had no appreciation of her reality?

For years, I struggled with my lack of involvement in mom's growing dependency. Today, I've accepted what happened. This was a perfect storm––a person who had addictive tendencies, a terminal illness, an enabling environment, a patient who had inherent fear of future unknowns, and a medical community that had yet to understand the importance of managing a patient holistically. It was what it was. Mom was addicted to Xanax, among other things. It's a part of her story. However, it doesn't diminish her as a person. She was beautiful, even if she didn't spend much time free of drugs.

### June 11, 1994

*I feel like I have been at Duke for two weeks. It will be one week tomorrow, but it seems much longer. I want to go home, but I also want to receive this treatment. Mom is really anxious to go home, and I think Ray is anxious for us to get home. I talked with Ray, Rick, and Rebecca this morning. Rick, Rebecca, and Brittany are in Knoxville for Link Hudson's wedding. Rebecca said Brittany missed me when she came into the house. I can't wait to see my family again. I miss them all.*

*I get the Adriamycin tonight. According to the nurse on shift today, I will be sedated before I get the big red stuff. She said I should sleep through the whole thing. I hope so.*

Adriamycin was the brand name for the generic drug Doxorubicin. Referred to as the "Red Devil," this drug gained a reputation as the harshest of all chemo treatments. The "devil" has been shown to kill cancer cells in all stages of their life cycle. Unfortunately, it also kills normal cells at an alarming rate. It has been found to be particularly toxic in heart tissue and leads to an increase in morbidity and mortality. This is some bad stuff.

I've had countless people tell me their doctor told

them there's no way they would give them this drug to treat their cancer. It's just too much.

I had no idea this was what mom was doing. I knew chemo was bad, and its reputation was nasty. However, I don't remember knowing how horrible her treatment was about to become. Looking back, this seems barbaric. I'm sure the doctors never said this, but it would've been accurate if they had said, "In an effort to give you time, we're going to unleash a clear red chemical in your body that will attack you. This will be the worst thing you've ever experienced. It might work." Seriously?

I don't know why I expect more, but I find it hard to believe that mom went into this moment understanding everything that was coming. Maybe she did. Maybe she was braver than I thought. After all, it's amazing what people will do to survive.

I hate cancer. I feel a visceral reaction to the very notion that it still exists, and that people must face the choices mom faced. Maybe it's better. Maybe advances have occurred, and the experience isn't so ghoulish. I don't know. I do know that the mortality rate for metastatic cancer hasn't changed materially in 20-plus years. Maybe the period from metastatic diagnosis to death is handled better. I hope that's true.

Today, the primary emphasis of breast cancer treatment is on early detection, which makes sense. When caught early, the risk of the cancer cells metastasizing is small, and long-term survival rates are very high. Credit should be given to the medical community for advancing to the point where a woman has a chance to impact their health before they face something so dreaded as a drug named the "Red Devil."

Despite the focus on prevention, there's still a gap. Roughly half the women in the US who are eligible for a mammogram don't get the screenings on schedule. This problem is worse in the underserved population. This means that statistically, women who are lower on the socioeconomic ladder experience higher levels of advanced breast cancer and the resulting challenges that come with advanced stages. In a country as wealthy as the US, it's embarrassing we can't find a way to invest in the lives of all people to ensure that we lower the percentage of humans who face the life that mom lived. We have to do better.

### June 12, 1994

*Well, I survived my first dose of Adriamycin. They gave me shots to help with nausea and to help me sleep. The medications did <u>really</u> well. I slept most of the night and didn't get sick. I actually feel pretty good today. I'm beginning to feel somewhat fatigued, but I am thankful to the Lord that I have not had any bad side effects. Mother and I had a good visit today. The nurse got her a more comfortable chair, and she looked a whole lot more rested when she left for the hotel tonight. I am really anxious to get through this and head home. I can't wait to see Ray. I can't wait to see home, and the garden, and flowers, and the pool. It will only be a couple more days.*

*Everyone here at the hospital has been great; they are all so nice and helpful. I am really lucky to be in this program.*

### June 14, 1994

*I am so happy I have finished my last chemo for this cycle, and I'm at the Brownstone Inn with mom. Tomorrow, we get to go back to beautiful Tennessee. I can't wait to see Ray, the home, my flowers, and garden, just everything. Everyone at Duke has been terrific. They are so professional, and I am so lucky to have been accepted into their program.*

Mom's writing reflects my recollection. Her attitude improved while she was at Duke. Despite the brutal Red Devil and all it brings, mom sounds more optimistic than she has at any other prior time. Her spirit, although tired, shines through. She's seeing things with hope and a stronger resolve.

It's ironic that at the very moment she's embarking on the hardest stretch of her treatment, her innate half-full personality is shining.

I remember the summer of 1994 fondly. Mom demonstrated a resolve and charm that brought me back to life before the madness started. However, my fears hadn't subsided. I still worried constantly. During this period, I called mom a lot. I wanted to check in on her and show her I cared, but it wasn't mom who gained the most from our daily chats. It was me. I'd call her, seeking to cheer her up, but she was the one who brought happiness to the call. She was engaged, attentive, and eager to bring a smile.

Mom had hope. She was capturing a bit of herself and sharing her mood with those whom she loved. It all combined to give mom strength to face daily misery with the positive mindset she held all her life.

A long, painful journey like the fight against cancer presents many ebbs and flows. It's easy to recall the worst of times and harder to relive the good times. Some of that has to do with volume. Usually, there are far more down than up moments, but there's more to it. Grief tends to overwhelm people. When grief is constant and seemingly unbreakable, it generates a sad status quo. No matter how hard you try, you can't escape the truth. You look at your loved one, and they look like a shell of themselves. It's sad, and it's hard to ignore. I always prepared myself before seeing mom, and yet, I was always taken aback by her appearance. The cancer was killing her, and her treatments were destroying her.

To this day, I can't look at pictures of mom taken while she was sick. Regardless of how hard she tried to smile, her gaze is pained. I look at her tortured expression, and I'm immediately crushed. It wasn't her. For years, the recurring image of her as a cancer patient haunted my memory. Whenever I allowed my mind to wander and remember how mom looked, I'd see her as a shrinking, pale, drawn-in, deeply tired patient.

Now I see mom, and the visual memories are changing for me. My time writing about her diary has been a mixed bag. To be sure, some of the memories are painful and initiate a sudden sadness. However, that feeling is fading from its previously dominant position.

This entry is a perfect example. Mom's daily existence was terrible, but she was still there, projecting her amazing energy. It was diminished, but it wasn't dead. She might not have looked like herself and couldn't do what she did before. She talked slower, laughed lower, and smiled with a forced grin,and her thoughts wandered, but she hadn't gone anywhere. I can draw comfort from her strength and peace when I think of her. Her willingness to fight offered me a life-sustaining gift, and I cherish it.

# CHAPTER 10

*July 19, 1994*

*Right now, I am sitting in a leather chair in Dr. Kerns' office taking chemo. The last month has been unbelievable. Somehow, I have managed to take all the chemo I was supposed to. I have suffered through all the side effects, mouth sores, fatigue, and pain from Neupogen, but I have had only one major illness event. About two weeks ago, I started running a temperature, chilling spells, and my white count dropped to 200, red count dropped, and I had a slight case of pneumonia. I ended up in the hospital, taking antibiotics, blood transfusions, and really cutting it close. I didn't realize it, but I had put myself in a position where I could have died. I just didn't realize it at the time. The past month has been a very bad time. I have been very sick most of the time for the past month. I go to sleep at night trying to escape it and wake up every morning thinking this day is going to be better, but it usually isn't.*

*This regimen of treatment leaves little time for recovery before you are taking another treatment. The side effects of this chemo change from day to day, except for the mouth sores. I know it is hard to understand, but mouth sores are so painful. It is necessary to take pain medication. Eating becomes such a painful chore that soon you would just as soon not eat.*

*I spent 12 days in the hospital with my pneumonia, low blood counts, etc. The last five days of that time, I was taking chemo. I learned a lot while staying in Parkwest Oncology. Death seems to be a word mentioned a lot. There does not seem to be a lot of enthusiasm and hope for life. So, needless to say, I did not like being in the hospital there. I WANT HOPE. That is why I am suffering through all of this. <u>None of this is fun. This is being done for the future.</u>*

*I see nurses shaking their heads about the treatment Duke has prescribed, but Duke is giving me hope. High doses of chemo and blood counts getting low seem to scare the nurses to death, but what scares me to death is not being here when my grandchildren grow up. So, this has been quite a month. I have suffered the whole month. There have been very few days since I have felt human, but I am making it, and I will continue to make it as long as there is hope.*

HOPE, A REASON FOR LIVING, and a mental toughness to fight––these qualities carried mom through the summer of 1994. Reading her diary leads me to two overarching conclusions: This period was awful, but we didn't completely appreciate it because mom was at her highest level of emotional toughness and was shielding her family from the details.

At no point during this summer did I internalize how bad her treatment was and how much suffering she endured. Whenever we spoke, she talked of hope and the future. She believed she was close to getting her bone marrow transplant and that it was going to alter her outcome. Her passionate desire to believe and her resolve to live for her family carried her. Duke obviously helped. They gave her a sense that she could trust in what they were doing.

As I read this, I wonder how mom's future would've been altered had she been resigned to receive care only at Parkwest Hospital. My sense is that she wouldn't have maintained her positive perspective and likely would've succumbed to the disease faster. There's no way to know that, but I believe that her attitude kept her going, and I believe she got strength from Duke.

However, it isn't fair to question the team at Parkwest. Working in a ward that reeks of death has to take a huge toll on the staff. It must be horribly difficult to convey hope when you've seen so many hopeless situations. Furthermore, being told to administer a treatment protocol that isn't your normal approach and seems extreme must add to the helplessness that the nursing team must have felt.

We're fortunate to have healthcare workers who sacrifice so much to provide for those who are at their worst. The recent COVID-19 pandemic underscores the uniqueness of these special heroes who go to work and interact with death all day, sometimes at their own risks. I don't know how they do it. I'm just grateful that they do.

I'm also grateful for the individual people who cared for mom. You don't get to thank them along the way, and you rarely get to thank them at the end. I hope they know how much the families of terminally ill patients appreciate them, and if they're faced with heated comments from a loved one, I hope they can forgive whatever is said. Death is emotional, and people say stupid things. I'm not aware of that ever happening with mom, but I also know we didn't get a chance to thank the team for their respectful care.

### July 24, 1994

*Today is Sunday night, and at this moment, I feel pretty good. Some days, it literally changes from hour to hour. Yesterday was a weepy day for me. I didn't feel good physically and emotionally, I was very low. I am getting really tired of feeling bad, and it seems I have nothing to look forward to except more sickness. I hear people talking about* vacations and going out to eat or going to the mountains, and I am very jealous. I know that I am fighting right now so that in a few months, I can be planning special events, but right now, all I have to look forward to this week is the hospital chemotherapy and maybe taking blood. I guess I am just on a pity party right now. I normally can keep my spirits up, but I am sure having problems doing that right now. I'm hoping that when the next three weeks are over, I may have a little rest before the bone marrow transplant.

I am going to try very hard to start doing some more positive things. I made a list this morning, and I am going to start writing short stories about things that have either happened in my life or things I have been told about. Maybe someday, the boys or maybe even the grandchildren will enjoy them.

I'm also going to start Christmas shopping so that if I feel good at Christmas, I can really enjoy Christmas instead of having to shop and wrap gifts. I'll be able to enjoy the decorations.

Please, dear God, forgive me for feeling sorry for myself. I know I have a horrible disease, but I am still very lucky. You have given me strength to get through this so far, and I have not been as sick as some people. You have also given me some of the best doctors who give me hope, and I am so thankful. Please, God, also be with Mr. Ramsey. He is very sick, but such a strong-willed person. Please help

*him enjoy his celebration of his anniversary. Be*
*with my family as they have to deal with me and*
*my illness. Thank you to all the people who have*
*come forward to give blood. I am so lucky. Keep*
*me strong, please. Amen.*

I wish she'd written those short stories. To my knowledge, she didn't. There isn't any evidence that she was able to write her memories down for us to enjoy. I've asked all my living relatives if they have anything like this from mom, and unfortunately, there seems to be nothing.

Even though I don't have mom's written words beyond this diary, this journey has motivated me to dig into my parents' past and family history. It's amazing how much you learn when you begin to explore. Makes you wonder why there were so many secrets. I don't know, maybe that's the norm for families. It certainly seems to be a pattern with mine.

For example, take my grandfather Tommy: I learned that he previously was married before he met mamaw. That brings up all kinds of questions. Are there unknown relatives out there? I'm told he didn't have kids with his first wife. Who knows. That was 90 years ago, so anything is possible. I gather mom didn't even know about her dad's first foray into married life. Somehow the secret was kept until recently.

My dad's side had an interesting secret I've learned about during this process. Based on what I've read, dad's mom and her siblings were convinced that their dad was Jewish. Evidently, he was fluent in Yiddish. I went back and looked at his pictures, and he was a striking-looking man who easily could've emigrated from Central Europe in the early part of the 20th century. The kids believed he kept it a secret because their mom wouldn't have married him if she'd known he was Jewish. I don't know if that's true, but I never expected mom's diary to lead me to discover that I might have Jewish blood.

I guess I understand why families keep secrets, sort of. However, it omits so much of what makes us who we are. Growing up, I didn't have a view that my family was special or even interesting; everything seemed so "normal." And it was, ironically because there were so many hidden things in our history that made us like everyone else.

I hate that I missed the chance to spend time understanding the stories and events that my parents and extended family experienced. For example, I didn't talk to either of my grandfathers about their time in the military during WWII. I don't believe either experienced combat, but they could've shared so much about the world as they saw it, had I taken the time to ask.

History is a grand thing and should be embraced. I'm writing the history of mom's cancer fight, but there was so much more to her life and those who were in her life. It frustrates me that I didn't take time to listen to their life stories. Maybe as I get older, understanding the past matters more to me. Or maybe I want to understand what makes me who I am. When mom was alive, I never thought I needed a connecting wire to who I was. When she died, the wire seemed severed.

Today, it doesn't feel so broken. I can't talk to mom, but her and her family's stories are bringing her back to life, and they're doing the same for me. It's so cool to write that because it's true. I'm not finished with her diary entries, and the remaining days she will chronicle are brutal. But like her positive view of her situation, I'm emboldened and reconnected with her and her family. Last week, I even got her secret recipe for banana pudding. It wasn't written down on a sheet of paper. Aunt Karen recited it from memory like she prepared it every other day. I can't wait to make it for my family and laugh wholeheartedly about the silly moments in my past that are resurfacing.

### *July 28, 1994*

*Well, I'm back in the hospital today to start my last chemo before going to Duke to have tests done to see if I'm better and when I'll get the bone marrow transplant. I really get aggravated at Parkwest Hospital. I have been here almost two hours, and all I have done so far is drink a cup of water, and I had to ask for that. No one has come in to check me in, say when I'm going to start my chemo or anything. And, of course, I am anxious to get started because the sooner I start, the sooner I get out of here on Tuesday.*

*Still no chemo, but the nurse came in and talked to me. I am determined this time to stay busier and not watch as much TV. I already have my puzzle out, and I am working on it. It sure keeps your mind busy and makes the time pass faster.*

*I had some scary news last night. A little girl at Vanderbilt was given the incorrect chemo and died. I know there is always the possibility of that happening. It just makes you realize how much you are at the mercy of other people.*

*Please, dear God, help the doctors find the right medication. Please find a solution for all those poor people in Rwanda. Don't let those children suffer any longer. Please help Rick and Rebecca as they try to arrange everything to build their house. Be with Mike as he tries to make a correct career decision. Help both my sons and their wives be good parents and raise their children to love you. Please be with Ray. help him recover from his knee problems and be pain free. Thank you for my mom and help her start back to rehab for many reasons, both physical and emotional. And please, dear God, help Jennifer find the right college to attend.*

Although she was mostly sweet as honey, mom had a feisty side. That trait was present in all the women in my family. My grandmothers, aunts, and cousins all possessed a Southern charm that could warm your heart and a temper that would grab your attention. Over the years, the world has come to know the expression, "bless your heart." I believed growing up and still do that women in the South use that phrase to express some displeasure while not showing their hidden intensity. It's the ladylike thing to do.

It was also used as a form of pity. Mom often would

say when she saw a plus-sized lady, "Bless her heart, she's big-boned." My aunt has shortened the phrase to "bless" when she sees or hears about someone who isn't at their best. I don't think they mean harm—call it empathy.

However, mom sometimes would cast aside her gentle demeanor for a more direct reaction. She was a tough advocate for dad when he was hospitalized with his various knee surgeries. I'd even say she was demanding. Not unlike most people, when it came to those she loved, she was ready to express herself.

In a strange way, I enjoy seeing mom complain about the hospital and her perception that they were moving too slowly. When you're expressing your anger about others, you're rarely throwing a pity party for yourself. Mom could be sulking, but she's not. She's annoyed. She's ready to get on with it. She clearly understands her goal and that delays aren't acceptable.

Her impatience also reflects her desire to get back to Duke, which represented hope. She was beginning to live at a higher level because of hope. I'm grateful that she had this brief period when she felt some measure of control.

As I noted before, mom lost her sense of control, partly because the disease and corresponding treatments took it from her, partly because of how we acted around her, and partly from our collective lack of understanding of how to act. Whatever the case, she suffered the darkness of losing control, and although she really didn't have control at this point in her journey, she felt like she did. She decided to go to Duke. She trusted them because they prescribed an aggressive course for her, and despite the local medical team's objections, she welcomed such treatments and was tolerating them. This was maybe the best period of mom's life after the cancer returned. It wasn't much, but it meant the world to her.

### July 30, 1994

*It's Saturday morning, and I'm still taking chemo. So far, the hospital stay hasn't been as bad. For one thing, I was in better shape when I came in. I am starting to feel tired, and I wake up during the night nauseous. I'm also handling it better because I brought more things to do, so time is passing faster, and I don't get depressed. I dread taking Adriamycin tonight. I am worried about the Adriamycin being mixed early this week. The pharmacist says the chemo is good through today, but I still worry. Ray is going to come and sit with me for a while this afternoon. He is meeting with Larry this morning. Hopefully they can get things worked out so he can get his deal. What a relief that would be. If this comes through, then we won't have to worry, and I can go on LTD.*

### July 31, 1994

*Even though I am in the hospital, this has been a pretty day. Ray came by and stayed with me for about three hours, and mom came by to see me for a while. I have also felt pretty good today. I was able to tolerate the Adriamycin last night, and I felt good today. Ray said everyone was asking about me at church, and David asked for a prayer for me this morning. That always makes you feel good to know people care so much.*

### August 2, 1994

*I get to go home today. I am about halfway through this. Now it will be on to Duke and testing to see where I fall in the categories and determine when I have my bone marrow transplant. I'm really going to be happy to get out of the hospital. There are some really sick people here this time. There are several that will probably not live to get out of the hospital, but that's what cancer is all about. You try, and you fight, but you know that you may be in their situation in the future. Cancer is truly a killer, and a very painful killer at that, but right now, I am just thankful I am doing well and hopefully on the road to recovery.*

*I had lots of good company yesterday. It helped my day pass fast. I also got calls from Karen and Mike.*

*I feel much better this time, so maybe I can do a few things while I am home.*

Mom finished the summer of 1994 on a high note. She received the aggressive treatments that Duke prescribed and tolerated them better than at any other time during her cancer years. Her attitude was strong, her spirit intact, and her outlook positive. She felt––we all felt––a sense of direction.

It was obvious then, and is more obvious today, that how a person views their situation determines how they react to it. I know that's easier said than done, and that you can't judge someone's response to a crisis. That's not fair, but it's encouraging to know that your outlook can help you get through bad times. I never directly questioned mom's reaction to her cancer, and I remain as impressed with her today as I was 25 years ago. She was strong.

Having the chance to reflect on the words she conveyed and my memory of that period gives me hope for my future. As you get older, it's natural to fear the unknown and worry about what will come. I've often thought about how I'd react to a medical scare. Mom offered me a reminder that how you view the world matters. Even in the worst of situations, and mom's was bad, your mind can help you.

At this point in mom's struggle, she had trouble walking. She lost an alarming amount of weight, her strength was gone, and her ability to do daily activities was all but taken away, yet she maintained enough gumption to handle the Red Devil and act like it wasn't so bad.

I'm proud of her and all the people who face the same type of challenges with dignity and grace. Recently I noticed an elderly woman walking through the lobby of a hotel where I was staying. She weighed less than 100 pounds, had lost her hair, was stooped over, used a cane, and yet smiled and chatted with every person she passed. I don't know her, don't know her story, but she's impressive, and I hope she has all the love and support she deserves and is blessed, whatever happens.

# CHAPTER 11

### *September 1, 1994*

*Well, it has almost been a month since I wrote, and a lot has happened. I took the last of my chemo. Ann called Duke, and they gave her the last test to be run. I finished the test in one week, and on Friday of that week, I got a call from Duke that said I had an appointment on the following Monday. They said I would only be here two days. Come on Monday and go home on Tuesday. But that quickly changed. On Monday, I was at the clinic at 4:30 to have blood drawn. The hotel took us on the shuttle to the hospital for scans and X-rays. We had no problem with the test, but couldn't get the shuttle to come pick us up. We had to wait 1.5 hours. I was so tired and so sick that as soon as I got back to the hotel, I had to go to bed. On Tues-*

*day, I went to the clinic for an examination and a biopsy. Dr. Rubin did the exam, then the biopsy, and this by far was the most painful. I thought I was going to die. He gave me some morphine before and after the procedure. Yesterday, I had to go to the clinic in the morning for cross-typing of blood. Afterward, I received two units of blood. This was the first blood I had received that wasn't donated by a designated donor. I just pray the blood was OK and not AIDS-infected. Today, I had no appointments, so mom and I went to Burlington and did some Christmas shopping. We got a lot done, and we had a good time. Now tomorrow, it's back to more testing and getting ready for the marrow harvesting. It's very possible I could have a transplant on September 16. I'm scared, but I know it has to be done. I have met some really nice people here. The people at the hotel are very nice. The people at the clinic are just super. They will do anything to make you comfortable and happy. I really hope everything comes through so I can go ahead and have the transplant and be well by Christmas. Sometimes I get a little chicken and want to wait a while, but deep down inside, I know that it's best to have it done now. I am fighting a real battle with depression, and I know mom is too. Ray is having a difficult time too. But when all of this is over, we will be better people for what has happened to us. The whole process is so overwhelming. We just have to get through it.*

## September 2, 1994

*Today was a big day. I was selected to have an immediate bone marrow transplant. I had four tests today, then came back to the hotel to wait for the results. Everyone I talk to is very happy and excited. I don't know if I am happy or not. I'm really scared and very tired of fighting this battle. I am thankful to have this opportunity to be cured. I'm also really anxious to get it over with. Maybe by November 1, I will be feeling better and can enjoy the holidays. and especially my family.*

## September 15, 1994

*Lots of things have happened since I last wrote. Besides a lot of tests, transfusions, etc., I had surgery last Tuesday for the bone marrow harvest. The next day, mother and I went back to Tennessee to get ready to come back to Durham. I had three-and-a-half days to spend with my family. Ray and I spent as much time together as possible, and Rick, Rebecca, and Brittany came up for a couple of days. It was a very emotional few days. It was tough saying goodbye to everyone, but especially to the kids and most of all, Ray. Mother and I came back to Durham Sunday. On Monday, I did pheresis and took two units of blood. It took all day Tuesday. I visited with Dr. Grant and did pheresis again. Yesterday, I had surgery to replace my Hickman catheter. Today was to be the day I rest, but instead, it was a day of worry and pain. My hip hurts and so does the spot where I had surgery. I am very tired of hurting and feeling bad, but tomorrow is the big day. Unless something happens, I will go into the hospital for the high-dose chemo. Maybe it will be over soon.*

*Dear God, please be with me and my family and friends during the next several days and weeks. I feel so weak. Please give me strength to withstand this. If it be your will, please help me get well. If not, please accept me into your kingdom. Amen.*

LIKE MOST EVERYTHING IN MEDICINE, the science surrounding bone marrow transplants and their use has changed dramatically. First tried in 1968, bone marrow transplants were intended to replace or cleanse damaged bone marrow. Specifically in cancer patients, bone marrow typically is damaged due to either the cancer attacking the cells or chemo treatments altering the cells or leaving them nonfunctioning.

Generally, heavy doses of aggressive chemo are administered to kill diseased cells and malfunctioning bone marrow. In mom's case, they applied this approach and gave her the "Red Devil." Prior to the transplant, they harvested her bone marrow and performed pheresis, a process of removing blood from the patient so that they could separate identified blood components such as platelets, plasma, etc. In the procedure, some cells are kept. The retained cells are "washed" in anticipation of returning them to the patient, thereby giving them productive bone marrow to produce healthy red and white blood cells.

Unlike today, when bone marrow transplants involve an outside donor who's a match and possesses healthy bone marrow, mom was donating her own marrow. The plan was to reinsert good marrow into her body in the hopes that the cleaned bone marrow would do its job. Sadly, that was all that was available at the time. I understand the attempt, but it seemed like a long shot. It was.

I don't know what the survival rate post-transplant was at the time, but I don't remember conversations from the physicians relayed to dad or any other family member indicating anything more than that this was the last chance to save her life.

Compounding the grim outlook was the reality of what mom was going to endure. The first step, attacking her cells with the "devil" to obliterate the bad cells, beat her down to her lowest level of strength and sustainability. Her body had lost all power to fight what was happening, and she was, at best, holding on. The removal of the bone marrow and replacement of "improved" bone marrow took a week and was exhausting. What followed was a long period trying to recover. Ever-present in her recovery phase was the very real risk of a bacterial infection that would kill her. Her body had no natural ability to resist an infection, as her white blood cells were depleted. She was at the mercy of fate, luck, and God.

I remember thinking how crazy this was. Mom said, "They're going to kill my immune system and put back better bone marrow, then I have to rebuild my system.

Hopefully, I won't die in the process." She was desperate, and this was a desperate attempt.

Today, bone marrow transplants are more targeted with donors and with what they're seeking to repair. As such, the results are better. The short-term danger is still present, but the long-term prognosis is more hopeful. I'm relieved to know patients today are not likely to face the odds and torture mom endured. So much was given for so little upside.

As good as the summer of 1994 was for mom and our family, the fall was a dark, sad time. Mom was quartered off in Durham, unable to connect personally with family and so miserably sick that she didn't want to engage by phone. It's hard to describe, but it felt like she left us. I don't know what I expected when it started, but I wasn't prepared for the abrupt change.

This was hard on dad, as he was totally unable to do anything. It was also the time when I think dad started to experience what his life would be like when mom was gone. He didn't like being alone. Mom was his best friend, and having her away for weeks on end was a stark view of what was to come. Years after mom passed, dad admitted that he didn't believe the transplant would work. He also said that no matter how hard he resisted, it was during this period that he started to say goodbye to her privately, in his own way.

Mamaw was in Durham with mom, and her burden was immense. I can't imagine, no matter the parent's age, how difficult it is to see a child pass away. Staring at them every day and knowing there isn't anything you can do but provide comfort and support is overwhelming. Mamaw did what she could, and she was amazing, but this took years off her life. From this point forward, she always looked tired and sad. She'd seen the up-close view of how bad mom was doing, and I'm sure she couldn't strike that from her memory.

As for mom, she was never the same, emotionally or physically, after the transplant. Even though she survived the procedure, I don't think she ever really recovered. Never again would she have a time like she did in the summer of 1994. Her light and attitude had faded forever.

I've often wondered whether it was worth it, or what mom would say about that question. Mom still had time before she passed, but her quality of life was impacted dramatically. I don't know how she felt, and it isn't for me or anyone else to decide. It was mom's choice and her right to determine her path and how she processed it. She never told me her opinion about the Duke transplant. I don't know whether her diary will offer insight. Whatever the answer, I couldn't have been prouder of her. She went to the depths of hell to beat cancer, and to live for her family. Regardless of the outcome, that's a noble, loving act.

# CHAPTER 12

## May 27, 1998

*Well, diary, it has been a long time since I wrote. Little did I know what I was facing when I wrote that I was going into the hospital for a high dose of chemo, and hopefully everything would be OK. Well, I obviously survived. There were times when I thought I wouldn't. I was so sick that at times I prayed to die. I was at Duke and very sick for almost two months. Mother was there with me taking care of me. She went to the clinic with me every day to see the doctor and get any treatment I needed. I took a lot of blood and platelets. I also took things like potassium, magnesium, etc. After the high-dose chemo in the hospital, I was released to a unit at a hotel where the entire top floor was for bone marrow patients. Mother and I stayed* *in a room with double beds. It had a microwave, small refrigerator. Mom, as my caretaker, was responsible for taking my temperature and my blood pressure. She also encouraged me to eat, but I just couldn't. She didn't always feel good, and I know she worried a lot. I was in a very serious condition, and she had a lot of responsibility. <u>Too much responsibility.</u> Every day, we went to the clinic, had a blood test, saw the doctor, then took whatever treatment necessary. Most of the rest of the day was spent in our hotel room. Sometimes I would go for a short drive. After a few weeks, my white count rose from 100 (which is what it was when I got out of the hospital). Ray and David Willingham came to visit me. I had no hair, and I was red and swollen for a couple of weeks. I had to take an antibiotic called vancomycin. The doctors did not know where the infection was coming from, but they suspected it was coming from my Hickman catheter. The antibiotic I was taking is, as far as I know, the strongest antibiotic you can take. I was very sick. I looked horrible. Ray later told me that he told David he did not think he would ever see me alive again. This was also a very bad time for Ray. He was by himself in Knoxville trying to take care of the house, worrying about finances, working and worrying about me. We talked to each other every night, but there were times when I didn't want to talk to him because I was so sick. I think I really hurt him by not talking to him. I tried to* *explain to him about how sick I was and how I didn't feel like talking. I love him so much, but I was just very, very sick. Ray and I have always loved sports. We have always enjoyed them together. One Saturday night, he called me, and he was very excited about the Tennessee game that day. He started telling me about the game. I told him I couldn't talk about football. I know it hurt him very much, but I didn't mean to. Ray, someday you will read this, and I want to tell you I'm sorry. I love you very much, but I was just too sick. I had no interest in anything except getting well and coming home. Not only was I very sick, but I was also very scared. I knew that if my temperature or blood pressure went up, mom had to call the hospital, and I would probably be admitted, and the thought of going back into the hospital petrified me. The isolation unit at Duke was like a sterilized isolation unit in prison. Also, if you needed to go back to the hospital, that meant you were very sick and probably in serious trouble. Don't get me wrong—the nurses, doctors and everyone at the medical unit were wonderful to all patients, and although the transplant did not work, I think it extended my life longer, and hopefully the doctors will have a cure very soon.*

*Mom and I continued a pretty regular schedule. Sleep as good as possible, shower, and mom would go downstairs for the continental breakfast. She would bring rolls and buns back. I would take this with me to the clinic. While I was taking treatment, I would do the best I could to eat as much as I could. Every two days, I would go in the clinic van to the hospital to have chest X-rays. Of course, it was very important that I did not get pneumonia. Mom could go with me. That was pretty much our routine for six weeks. We were watching the blood counts and especially for my platelets to rise. Until that happened, I could not go home. I must be at the clinic until I did not have to take transfusions. One day, two nurses came running in my room after I had my blood test. They were so excited. I had two platelets on my own without a transfusion. This meant I was close to coming home to Tennessee. What a happy and exciting day. I got to go home two days later, and I immediately had to go to the doctor the day after I got home and have a transfusion of platelets. But that was the best transfusion I have had. I don't know what the date was, but it was the last week in October 1994.*

*Unfortunately, the transplant was unsuccessful. The cancer came back, and since then, we have watched carefully for new spots. When found, we normally radiate and use chemo. It has been very important to keep the cancer in my bones. If the cancer gets in my organs, the cancer will spread faster, and I will not live long. Immediately after returning from Duke, I was very sick just trying to recover from the transplant. I slowly regained* some energy, but I am very far from feeling normal. Chemo, radiation, medication, etc., keep me pretty well down, but I have my good moments. I have a hard time working. My right leg is pretty well gone. It is very weak. I stay fatigued most of the time. But I am still alive, and my quality of life is pretty good. I must continue to fight until they get a cure for this horrible disease.

Most of my time is spent at home. I do some housework, but not a lot. Ray helps me a lot. Of course, he does all the outside work, and he and mom help me buy and carry the groceries. I could not take care of myself without help. There are times when I am too weak to drive. Shopping is something I cannot do. For the past two or three years, I have given money to the boys and their families, and I do the same for Pam and Karen, and they do the Christmas shopping for me.

Ray and I seem to be closer now than ever. We have always had a very strong marriage, but it is even stronger now. He has been very understating and wonderful during this whole mess. Some of the things we have always done together I can't do now. I have been able to go to about two football games a year, no basketball games, and very few baseball games. I can't walk very far, then I get tired so quickly. Ray has been real understanding. He just gets on the phone and finds someone else to go with him.

*Mom has had health problems also. She had bypass surgery. I felt so bad because I could do very little to help. Karen came and stayed a couple of days, Pam stayed with her a couple nights and when mom came home, Aunt Pauline came and stayed for a week, then Aunt Nita came and stayed for a few days. Without everyone's help, I don't know what I would have done. Aunt Becky also came a while.*

*Ray also has had two surgeries since I got the cancer. With one, I stayed with him. With the other, I couldn't. I felt so bad. He stayed by himself and did OK, but I really felt awful that he was by himself.*

*During late 1997, tumors appeared in my shoulders, one elbow, and a spot on my skull. I had radiation for two weeks, and after the first of the year, I started chemo. I have been sick since January. Bronchitis, sinusitis, side effects from chemo. At the present, I cannot take chemo because my blood levels are too low. The chemo was just too strong. Now my biggest problem is fatigue caused by the low blood and platelet counts. It is just a matter of resting and eating properly so I can get back on treatment before the cancer spreads.*

*Ray and I are going on vacation this year. We are going to Jamaica with Rick and Kimberly. I just hope nothing happens to spoil this.*

A LMOST FOUR YEARS BETWEEN DIARY ENTRIES. I admit that this break catches me by surprise. I assumed when I started reading her diary that the pace would be reasonably consistent. Obviously, I was wrong. Her comments above offer few specifics about the interval, but her almost nonchalant reference to the transplant's failure provides all the context needed for the four-year gap.

Almost immediately after she settled back in Knoxville, the cancer showed it hadn't gone anywhere. In fact, the tumors' prevalence in her bones seemed to accelerate. Mom was a terminal cancer patient, with a very painful version of cancer, who regularly took radiation and chemo to slow its progression. Her life became nothing but a survive-and-advance mindset. No longer was there hope for remission. Her cancer was relentlessly attacking her, and the doctors had run out of options to change the outcome.

Mom's days revolved around constant pain from the disease, treatments that were miserable, and a significant reliance on pain meds. Four years, four long years of nothing but pain, doctors, and a cloud of pending death hanging over you. I don't blame her for wanting to escape reality. I would've wanted the same.

Today, when a patient is deemed terminal, hospice care is offered to the patient, and support is provided for the family. It's a caring, respectful approach given to a patient, helping them leave this world in the most dignified way possible. Whether it's home care or at a hospice facility, the patient is afforded a chance to pass away under the oversight of experienced healthcare providers who understand, among many things, how to ensure that the patient doesn't suffer.

Explicit in hospice care is the understanding that any attempts at treating the disease will be discontinued.

Mom's situation was the worst of all possible scenarios. She was dying, but she wanted to continue to seek care, and she was in enormous pain––pain that had she been in hospice would've been managed effectively.

Month after month, the doctors identified new tumors or noticed existing ones regrowing, and they would radiate them and give her chemo. Imagine doing that for four years. I can't now, and I couldn't process it then. I wondered why mom didn't accept her fate. How could she continue to repeat this horrible process? Somehow, she did, but she was completely gone.

Her need to take pain meds and Xanax, along with her self-administration of the meds, created an untenable situation. It's hard to describe the feeling of knowing she's suffering horribly, while simultaneously having the sense that she was out of control. I've never felt so helpless and inadequate.

I tried everything I could to explore how to help mom change the course she was on. I failed every time. I distinctly recall thinking that maybe she needed to know it was OK to accept her fate and that we were proud of her. Maybe if she knew she could let go, she would.

I sought counsel from friends who had experienced this moment with a parent and thought carefully about how to address my concerns with mom. Eventually, I got the courage to talk to her about it. It wasn't easy.

With apprehension, I drove to mom and dad's house for the day. When I got there, mom was sitting quietly in her recliner staring blankly at the wall. I couldn't tell whether she was medicated or just in a daze, but she hardly acknowledged me when I sat down. Needing to feel closer, I moved a dining room table chair and positioned it right in front of her. She smiled, and her face began to brighten.

We talked softly for a few hours about nothing in particular. As time passed, mom seemed to be more engaged and connected to what we were discussing. Sensing she was listening, I asked, "Can we talk about something?" She made eye contact and said of course. "Mom, you've fought this like no one ever could've imagined, and because of that, Ashley and Brittany know who you are, and we have had an additional five-plus years together. I wonder, though, if it isn't time to stop putting yourself through this. It doesn't seem like a way to live." She stared at me for what seemed like forever. Slowly, she said, "Mike, I don't want to die, but I'm not afraid to die. I want to see my kids and grandkids do more. I haven't had enough time yet."

It's hard to know what to say to that, but I wanted to add one more thing. "Mom, you take a lot of medicine, and it worries me. I understand why you do it, and I want you to know we do not want you to suffer. But you need to understand that your need to medicate has eliminated any ability to do anything beyond sitting in that chair. If the pain is too much, then please allow yourself to go peacefully. You don't have to fight for us. You need to do what's best for you."

She thanked me and asked me to give her a hug.

I've thought about that moment since the day it happened. I didn't accomplish what I wanted. My goal was for mom to stop putting herself through a living hell. In that regard, I failed. She never stopped fighting and was fighting on the last day; however, some things changed after that chat. She adjusted her pain medication use. From that moment forward, mom made it a point to not be as medicated when she was with the family. I guess you could say that's good, but it made me feel guilty and ashamed. Mom was in enormous pain. How could I have given her the impression that I wanted her to stop easing that burden? I know she wanted to be with the kids and grandkids, and we did get more time together. However, I hate to think of how awful she must have felt and the sacrifice she made to put on a good face, just so she could be with us.

### June 17, 1998

*Ray and I drove to Nashville last week. We spent the night at Rick's apartment, then we headed to Tunica. We spent the weekend eating great food, playing slot machines, and just visiting. We came back on Monday after a really great weekend. We had a lot of fun, and I was really pleased with my stability. I walked more and seemed to have more energy. I was really pleased because I want to feel good when we go to Jamaica. Since we got back Monday, I have been to the doctor twice for shots* and basically rested.

## June 20, 1998

Yesterday was our 33rd wedding anniversary. We didn't do anything extra special. We are going out tonight. We decided to combine Mother's Day, Father's Day, and our anniversary and celebrate by buying things for our trip. Mom is going to Karen's house tomorrow. I'm glad she is going. She needs to get out of this house. It will be good for her.

## June 24, 1998

Well, we didn't have anything planned for our anniversary, but our kids and family sure did. Rick and Kimberly, and Mike and Tiffiny asked whether they could have a small party at Willie's house. It turned out to be larger than they thought. They invited 40 people, expected about 20 to show up, and about 35 came. We were surprised and happy. We had friends and relatives from Knoxville and Murfreesboro, South Carolina, Nashville, Tellico Plains. Some of them we hadn't seen in a long time, so it was really great. We got lots of beautiful gifts, but most of all, we had lots of beautiful friends and family.

Rick, Kimberly, and Brittany stayed with us Saturday and Sunday. On Monday, I got sick and started vomiting. Yesterday, I went to the doctor for a shot of red blood cells. I still don't feel good today, and it is Wednesday.

*Please, dear God, please help me feel better for Ray's sake more than mine. He wants to spend time together, and it seems every time we have an opportunity, I get sick. Please, God, help me feel better soon.*

The anniversary celebration was a beautiful and sad event. As a family, we decided to have the gathering because we didn't feel mom would make another anniversary. There was no way they would reach 35 years (a more typical date to mark with a party), and next year seemed like a big stretch, so we went for it.

The party was attended by a long list of mom and dad's friends. Three decades of memories crammed themselves into the house. However, gone was the normal jovial silliness that characterized mom and dad when they were around loved ones. It was more somber. It didn't feel like a wake, but it was close.

I still can see mom sitting in the center of the room talking individually to each guest. I think she was happy, but it was hard to tell. Frankly, even though it was intended to be a special evening, and it was, my memory of the day is dominated by sadness. Twenty-five years later and I can't shake the image of mom. She was beautifully dressed and lovely as always, but she was so sick.

I'm glad to hear mom felt this was a special moment. I'll use her words to try to retrain my brain to think more positive thoughts about the party, but it'll be hard. It was every bit as sad as her funeral. Maybe more so.

This was mom's last diary entry.

# PART III

# CHAPTER 13

I N THE SIX YEARS SINCE MOM was first diagnosed with breast cancer, her life was altered so much as to be unrecognizable from her healthy years. A life-threatening disease has a way of doing that. It also can force you to reflect on your history. As mom entered the waning months of her life, she wanted to recall better times, and there was a lot to draw from.

Mom was a joyful person, full of laughter and mischief, a product of a family that loved to turn every event, good or bad, into a time to gather, share hope, and love. There was always humor in every aspect of her life. It's an impressive trait to be able to face all challenges and heartaches cheerfully. Mom and her family could do that.

As the summer of 1998 faded to fall, mom began to share memories from her past. It was a special time, filled with laughter, tears, and sadness. Mostly, though, it was a gentle journey, through mom's eyes, retelling her story as she spun it.

Like the time mom talked about the struggles with her weight. This was her lifelong challenge. I never recall a time when mom wasn't trying to drop pounds, and it wasn't easy. Food was a big part of her heritage, happiness, and how she entertained, and the food wasn't necessarily healthy. In fact, almost everything we ate growing up is now identified as things to avoid. I'm told that every time you eat a hot dog, it takes a few minutes off your life. Maybe, but they're worth it, and we ate them all the time.

As we talked, mom reminded me that she tried every diet she'd ever heard of and joked that she was a lifetime member of Weight Watchers––having proven this by losing weight and gaining it right back. She recalled her anticipation every morning stepping on the scale to see whether she dropped a few pounds, only to be disappointed that the late-night ice cream probably didn't help her daily goal. She was poking fun at herself, and it was cute. After a while, her voice trailed off, and she said, "I guess I was big-boned too."

Mom felt jovial and seemed to be relishing telling me vignettes that I hadn't heard. She sheepishly asked, "Can I tell you a secret?" "Of course," I said. "Don't tell your dad, but I got tipsy with Tiffiny." To my knowledge, mom never drank, and I know dad was strongly against drinking. He had bad memories from his childhood being around family members who were drunks who became scary when they got lit. Considering dad's demands that he and mom never drink, I understood why she didn't want me to say anything to dad, but I was surprised I'd never heard the story before.

"After you and Tiffiny moved to Rome, Georgia, we came to visit," mom said. "I think it was our first visit. While you guys were watching the Braves on TV, Tiffiny and I went out back on the patio to chat. I didn't notice it at first, but Tiffiny had a pitcher in her hand. Turns out it was margaritas, and they were good." She then smiled the happiest of smiles.

"How tipsy did you get?" I asked. "Very," she replied.

Mom and I laughed hard as she recalled all the silly things she said while Tiffiny topped off her glass. Turns out, she always wanted to drink alcohol and couldn't. It took my new wife to sneak off with her and give her a taste.

"Did you ever have another drink?" I wondered.

"I'd slip away and have a nip every once in a while," she answered with a mischievous smile.

Mom wasn't particularly athletic, but she loved sports. When she did try to be athletically active, mishaps occurred, like the time she hit Karen's husband, Levourn, in the leg with a wayward golf shot. I'm told it hit him squarely in the back of the knee. Levourn fell over like a soccer player in the World Cup, seemingly dying. No one came to his aid; they were too busy laughing at the absurdity of mom hitting him as he stood at a 45-degree angle to the tee box. I asked mom to tell me about it, and she said, "It was the only shot that day that I got off the ground."

Mom couldn't swim and was terrified of putting her

head below the water. In all my life (and we had a pool in our backyard), I never saw mom submerge her head. It's bizarre to think she never learned. She spent the early years of her life in the country, and yet never picked it up. She was a wimp around water, but she was always near it. I asked her whether she ever wanted to learn how to swim, and she responded emphatically, "No." I let it go, but teased her relentlessly. Nonplussed, she never took the bait or attempted to learn. She liked standing upright in the pool, and that was as far as she was going to go.

Mom had a beautiful voice, and I fondly remember her listening to Dolly Parton and Elvis on the record player, singing loudly to "I Will Always Love You" or "Suspicious Minds." What I didn't know was that when she was in high school, she was a member of a traveling quartet, along with her dad and close friends Junior and Josephine Jinx. Mom sang alto for the group, and papaw sang bass. They performed at church revivals. After marriage, mom didn't continue to sing in public, but she belted out tunes each morning as she made breakfast. In Knoxville, there was a daily variety show that aired early each weekday, "The Cas Walker Show." Cas carried on with a bunch of foolishness and frequently hosted local musicians on the show. I distinctly remember mom turning on our little black-and-white TV in the kitchen. She laughed at the show's silliness and always found a way to croon along with the guest to a favorite song. Starting the day with laughter was the perfect tonic for mom. She worked hard and was beginning a day that included her job as a parent, her work, and the expectations she understood as a wife, but she did it with a smile.

Speaking of breakfast, mom rose every day and made a spread, without fail—eggs, bacon, and biscuits and gravy were served. I always went to school full, and it was a point of pride for her. So, it was a shock for me the first time I spent the night at a friend's house and realized cereal and milk were the only things served. How could anyone reasonably expect to function during the day without a full breakfast?

Leaving the house undernourished wasn't a problem for me. Mom and her breakfast always held a special place in my heart. It started the day with a personal dose of love that only a mom could give. To this day, I make a large breakfast each Saturday morning, and I welcome others to join. It's a nod to mom and the thousands of Southern breakfasts she served.

Mom was getting weaker in the fall of 1998, and I was spending more time trying to connect. These moments increasingly were heartbreaking, but sometimes mom pulled me up from our misery and shined a beacon of light. No time captures that more than the day she asked me to give her eulogy. I never thought about it and was hard-pressed to know how to respond. I weakly said "yes" and quickly sought to change the subject. Mom would have none of that.

She said, "Listen to me," so I nodded.

"I want you to say something on my behalf."

With a big smile on her face, she said, "During the eulogy, make eye contact with your dad. Tell him I have a message for him. Tell him I hope he remarries and finds happiness. Tell him that's my wish, but also tell him that when he goes to bed at night, know that I'll be sitting on the bedpost watching him. I hope he has fun."

She laughed so hard, I thought she was going to break her fragile ribs. She promised me not to tell anyone in advance what she wanted, and I didn't. I also did what she asked. You should've seen the look on the faces of a church full of Southern Baptists and Presbyterians. It was priceless. Dad laughed quietly. He knew exactly what she would've wanted and would've said.

Mom and dad made the trip to Jamaica with Rick and his second wife, Kimberly. I don't know how they were able to go. Mom barely could walk, and she was frail and vulnerable. However, she was adamant they were going to go. There are many pictures from the trip, and in all of them, mom is smiling and appears happy. Rick said the trip was challenging and offered little solace. I'm glad they went, though. Mom wanted to continue to live as best she could.

Mom and dad didn't travel much. In fact, I believe this was the only time they ever left the US. Dad was a bit of a home body. He was happiest when in Knoxville. Mom wanted to see the world, but dad won out, and they stayed close to home. I asked mom after she got back from her trip what she thought. She was interested to see how people lived, fascinated by the local culture, and grateful she made the trip. I could tell it was important for her, and there was more on her mind. I asked, "Are there other places you would've wanted to visit?" She said, "I grew up in my small little world, and I always wanted to see beyond my life. I wanted to travel everywhere. Europe was on my wish list. Specifically, Scotland and Ireland. I also wanted to go to the Far East." She paused for a moment before continuing. "But you know, I wouldn't change anything. I'm so happy with my life and all the things I was able to do."

Her sincere comment about her life was comforting. She was satisfied and didn't have an envious desire to see something she missed. But she did have a request: "Mike, make me a promise––go and do what you want. See the world. You and I are alike; you've always been like me. I know you view the world in a hopeful, interesting way. Go enjoy it and learn from every experience you have."

I privately lived with that admonition and pursued alternative travel and experiences. It has been a blessing for me and a gift to my kids. They've done and seen things that have altered how they view life and others. Maybe I would've engaged in my active pursuit of travel without mom pointing me in this direction, maybe not. I don't know, and it doesn't matter. What I do know is that every time I'm in some unique corner of the world, I pause for a moment and connect with mom. I feel the need to have her with me, and through my own meditation, I believe she's there.

The most memorable example of this occurred during a trip I took in 2013. I was on the Orient Express traveling from Venice, Italy, to Stockholm, Sweden. It was stunningly beautiful, and all the things you might imagine it to be. But what I'll never forget is the first night. We were lumbering across Germany, and it was a little past midnight. Tiffiny and I joined a small group of friends in the bar car for a cocktail. In the car, there was a grand piano and a musician playing tunes to pass the time. I was feeling nostalgic and trying to connect with mom when the pianist suddenly began to play "Tennessee Waltz." I placed my drink on the coffee table and began to weep quietly. I already was overwhelmed to be so blessed to be on this fabulous trip, on the ornate Orient Express, then home and my family came pouring into my mind. It was a moment I'll never forget and always will cherish. No matter where you wander, you're never far from where you came from. It's comforting and reassuring. It's also a blessing.

As the fall of 1998 progressed, mom receded farther into her cocoon. There wasn't much left in her, and she ran out of ways to fight. Only time and pain remained. For dad, this was a particularly brutal period. He was helpless, heartbroken, and lonely. He, too, was watching the passage of time. He already had said goodbye to his wife of 33 years, had watched her suffer, and secretly wanted her misery to end. He never said that out loud until years later. He wasn't ashamed to have reached that point, just destroyed by the fight.

I think mom had an inkling of this. In December, Tennessee won the SEC and was selected to play Florida State in the National Championship game in Tempe, Arizona. Watching Tennessee play for a football championship was a lifelong goal of dad's, and he wanted to be there, but wouldn't leave mom. Mom called me and asked me to take him, and if necessary, force him to go.

He was reluctant, but we went. During our time out West, dad never once talked about mom. It was notable that he chose not to discuss her at all. He was tired. He needed a break and was unable to stir any emotions. We had fun, but it was subdued. As we flew home, I was keenly aware that dad thought mom's days were numbered. I didn't know what to say, so I said nothing. We separated in the Atlanta Airport, each heading to different connecting flights, both believing the next time we saw each other would be at mom's bedside.

But that wasn't to be. Even though mom was unable to function, she was unwilling to let go. She stopped receiving treatment, but she didn't stop fighting. It was admirable, but it was profoundly sad. At different times, I'd say to her, "It's OK. You've fought and given us seven years with you. My kids know and love you. You've achieved what you wanted to do." But mom was stubborn, and she held on, for weeks, then months.

# CHAPTER 14

THE SPRING AND SUMMER OF 1999 were unremark-
able. Life didn't change for mom, nor for all of us
who loved her. Her pain level was increasing, the cancer
was spreading, and time was running short, yet also
dragging on. It's difficult to explain, but waiting for a
terrible event to occur, you know you can't stop, and it's
stressful and draining. It was for mom, and it was awful
for dad.

I felt so sorry for both of them. Any remnants of their
prior life were gone. Mom was at home waiting to die.
Dad was watching this and praying for a peaceful end.
Sounds morbid, and on some level, it was. More than
anything, it was pitiful.

Rick and I visited mom often. From my perspective,
it always felt like I was going to ensure that I saw her
before the end. It was as though I was there for one last

visit. It's weird, though. After you do that a few times, you're not sure what the message or interaction should be. It was like I said goodbye several times, only to come back a few weeks later and do it again. After a while, I stopped that. I came as often as before, but the emotions of acting as though it was the end stopped. It was better for me and for mom.

It also was challenging to process when I wasn't with mom. Friends and extended family would call or ask how mom was doing out of concern or respect. I appreciated the questions, but after a while, I was tired of the constant inquiries. They meant no harm, but for months, the story was the same: "She's doing well." "She's fought a good fight." "I think the end is near." What else could I say? How long could I keep saying this?

There wasn't anything the doctors were doing to prolong her life, and actually gave her a life expectancy range, which she exceeded. She was living because she refused to die. It was remarkable. The doctors told dad they hadn't seen anyone fight so hard to live. I often wondered whether there was a backstory or something I didn't know. Recently, I learned there was.

Mamaw had been with mom, as her primary caregiver, since the original diagnosis. She lived with her in the room at Duke and witnessed every horrible step of the journey. Mom was her oldest child, and they were close. All of that was obvious and known. What I didn't know was that as mom teetered on the brink of dying, mamaw began to say to mom, "Please, don't leave me, please. I can't go on without you." For mom, this was all she needed to hear. As a lifelong pleaser, she had one last chore to do. That was to not leave her mother.

On the second Thursday of November, I woke up with a funny feeling. I didn't know what was driving me, but I knew I needed to go see mom immediately. I lived in South Carolina, so mom was three hours away, but it didn't matter. I cleared my schedule and drove to Knoxville. When I arrived at mom and dad's house, mom was sitting in the dark in her recliner gently rocking back and forth. On this day, mom seemed particularly out of it. I assumed she was on a heavy dose of meds, so I didn't comment. We chatted all day about nothing of substance, and her confused communication never abated. She wasn't logical and at times didn't seem to know where she was. We were together, but it was awful. I hated seeing her like this, and I felt sick to my stomach. I tried all day to engage to no avail. Mom wasn't coherent.

As the day drew to a close, I gave mom a big hug, told her I loved her, and got in the car to drive home. I was distraught and hated everything about what I'd just seen. I was mad at cancer, mad at the doctors, and mad at dad, mamaw, and me. I was just pissed. When I got home, all I could do was go to bed. I didn't talk to anyone, nor share my thoughts. I didn't know what to do or say. I was under tremendous pressure in my job and was about to embark on a one-week road show to raise $30 million-plus for the company I was CEO of, HomePoint. My mind wasn't right, and I was a jumbled mess. The trip was to begin on Sunday, and I couldn't get the scene of what I just witnessed out of my mind.

After an unproductive day of work, I got a call from dad. He said we needed to get to the hospital. He told me mom had fallen Thursday morning at around 3 a.m. and hit her head. He said the fall was bad enough that it had dented the drywall in the bathroom. She got up and didn't have her cane and somehow fell. He didn't tell me about it when I got to Knoxville because he didn't think anything was wrong, and mom wasn't complaining about it. But something was wrong.

Mom had hit her head so hard, she was bleeding in her brain. Dad said that when she got delirious, he took her to the ER, and after a few tests, the doctors came in and said to call the family. Mom was on her last leg. They couldn't stop the bleeding without surgery, and the outcome of that wouldn't be good, so it was time to say goodbye.

It was late, and the kids were asleep, so I told dad we'd be there first thing the next morning. As I hung up the phone, I realized mom wasn't high on Thursday; she was hurt. If dad had told me what had happened, I would've reacted differently, but it wouldn't have changed anything. I would've just preferred to have known.

Driving to Knoxville was the most surreal experience of my life. Seven years of watching mom fight, struggle, suffer, and fade had filled my head with emotions, and tears were falling. I was trying so hard to recall mom before this journey, but the sadness of this experience dominated my thoughts. The kids were quiet, as they never experienced a family death. Tiffiny was supportive, but none of us knew what we were going to see when we got to the hospital.

As soon as we arrived, I saw dad talking to the doctor in the hallway outside mom's room. I walked up, and dad introduced me. The doctor continued with me present. From his perspective, there was nothing that could or should be done. Mom's bleeding brain couldn't be controlled. "She won't make it through the day; let me know if you need anything." And with that, he was gone.

Dad and I hugged. I asked him if he was OK, and he shook his head yes. He looked tired and distant. All the years were culminating today, and there wasn't any emotion left. Dad looked at my family, and with a soft smile said, "Go in and see mom."

The room was small, or at least it seemed small. There were a lot of people in the room. I can't recall who was there. I just remember that the room was full, and everyone was wearing their favorite orange Tennessee shirt. It was Saturday in November, and the Vols were playing football at Arkansas. I know it's strange, but where I come from, college football is important. Wearing your game day shirt on a football Saturday is what people do. Even if it's to go to the hospital to see somebody before they die.

Mom looked asleep, but she wasn't. She was unconscious. She had an IV, but that was the only sign she was in a hospital room. The only goal the medical staff had was to support her transition and ensure she didn't suffer. I felt the instant pressure of everyone in the room turn their gaze at me. I was the oldest in that generation of the family and bore that load. I always hated the sense that I was somehow a leader over my brother and cousins.

Maybe it was self-imposed, but I don't think so. It seemed to happen and never stopped.

I nodded to everyone quickly and walked over to mom's bedside. I whispered that I was there and that I loved her. I reached out and grabbed her left hand and put it into my palm. Slowly I rubbed the top of her hand. Mom didn't respond. There wasn't any activity that indicated she knew I was there or what was happening. This went on for several hours. I don't remember much conversation among the gathered group. I was focused on mom and nothing else.

After lunch, the Tennessee football game started. Predictably, the TV was turned on and tuned to the game. This didn't create added conversation or any reaction, but all in the room watched intently. Turns out, it affected mom. Out of the blue, she opened her eyes and smiled at me. I was so excited to see her eyes and reached over to kiss her. She looked at me, then looked up at the TV. In a move that only mom could make, she asked, "How is the defense playing?" Stunned, I replied, "They're playing great." She smiled and responded, "I'm not surprised. Coach Chavis is a good coach."

I recognize that to most of you, this is an odd story, but in my family, it seemed normal––and for mom, in character. She found happiness in everything she could. Even though she was on her deathbed, she was seeking something to point to that wasn't sad. It was so mom. In the last moment she spoke to me, she was conveying a deeper message--march on, all is good. Admittedly, I didn't immediately get her agenda, but later, as I reflected, it was obvious. In the 32 years she guided my life, she always found a way to steer me toward optimism and hope. She preached the need to find happiness amid the travails of life. She believed it, even at the end of her own life.

Mom didn't die on that Saturday, though. The doctor said she was still fighting. The day ended, and I was faced with a horrible dilemma. I was expected to fly to Baltimore on Sunday morning for the national road show. It had been planned for months, was critical to our company's survival, and I was the CEO. The company had over 200 employees who were depending on me to do my job. I was stuck in the worst possible place: Leave for the good of the company, employees, and their families and miss the moment mom died, or stay for mom and put the company at risk of running out of money.

Dad told me that mom would've wanted me to do my job because people were counting on me. Everyone present said the same thing. Tiffiny was loving and comforting, and told me she supported whatever I chose to do. I was in a daze. I don't remember the moment when I actively made the decision. I just acted. At the end of the day, I asked if I could spend a few minutes alone with mom, then I left.

My final minutes with mom aren't memorable to me. I was numb. I don't even recall what I said. It doesn't matter, I think I'd said everything before. I kissed her on the forehead and slowly walked out. Tears overwhelmed me as I entered the hallway. Those outside walked toward me to console me, but I couldn't handle it. I softly brushed them aside and walked to my car.

On Sunday morning, the doctor told dad that mom was fighting and was obviously going to keep fighting. He said she was distressed, and that this was unnecessary. He said I know it's hard, but that you need to tell her it's OK to let go and pass on. Dad called me and told me about his conversation and said he agreed. It was time for mom to stop fighting. I thanked him for calling and cursed myself for not being there to help.

All that day, I was told that each loved one who visited mom told her it was OK to stop fighting. Dad said he spent time with mom trying to soothe her and comfort her. Nothing seemed to work.

Monday morning, more than 96 hours after her fall, mom lingered. The floor nurse asked whether there was anyone who could tell her it was OK to give up. Karen and Pam were there and started to wonder, "Do you think mom could talk to Pat?" They both knew mamaw previously had cried to mom and pleaded for her not to leave her.

Karen called mamaw, who was at home and an emotional wreck. Karen told mamaw what was going on. She asked, "Can you do this?" Mamaw said she could. Karen, responded, "If you can't, don't come to the hospital."

They say life isn't fair, and for mamaw, this was the most bitter of endings. She invested every ounce of energy she had to care for mom, and I'm certain never regretted a second of it. The love that a parent feels for a child is hard to measure. Most parents would give their life for their child, and I'm sure mamaw would've gladly taken her place, but that wasn't an option. Her only choice was to be there and never waver. And she did that.

I admire her for her love and sacrifice, and I'm grateful she cared for mom. It wasn't always perfect, and the combination of their similar personalities, clinical depression, and need to medicate contributed to how mom responded to her illness. However, that's quibbling. Mamaw was an amazing soul, and she should be honored and forever respected.

I don't know how, but for seven years, mamaw was able to maintain her strength. She was rarely alone and likely unable to release emotions. When you're caring for a patient, it's best if you hold it all in. You don't want to let the patient see that you're afraid or concerned. Imagine always having to be sharp and never letting your guard down while you watch your daughter fade. I can't, but mamaw did it.

Mamaw arrived at the hospital, and she did what was asked. I know it was a horrible task for her. It was the last thing she would've wanted to do, but she did it, and I'm eternally grateful for her loving action.

Shortly after mom heard those words from mamaw, she grew peaceful, her skin color became dove white, and her breathing slowed. Within 15 minutes, mom passed away. She was 53.

Mom never wanted to disappoint. Even when facing death, she held on because she didn't want to do something to hurt her family. It now makes perfect sense to me. Without knowing the final detail of mamaw's intervention, I spent years trying to square the delay between her fall and the time of her death. I knew she was tough, but I also knew she was tired and ready. What I didn't know was that her mother had asked her for something, and she was going to try everything to do what she was asked. It wasn't about her. It never was. Her whole life was about bringing joy to others. She was the consummate pleaser.

# CHAPTER 15

WHEN I LEARNED OF MOM'S PASSING, I was devastated. I was unable to control my tears, and my body shook violently. I wanted to throw up. How could I have missed her death? What was I thinking? I was so angry at myself, I was inconsolable.

It couldn't have been easy on the handlers who were shepherding me around the country for my countless meetings. I was the point person for this week, and their expectations were that I'd perform at a high level and deliver. We had been prepping for these meetings for weeks, and the time was now.

I didn't care at all about any of their stated or unstated expectations and was oblivious to what they said or any feedback I was given. They were of no consequence to me; however, I was hyper-focused on accomplishing my goal. I told myself I had to exceed the goal. If somehow

I failed at my task while also missing my mom's death, I'd never be able to live with myself. I had no choice. I had to get it done.

The constant refrain from everyone I spoke with was that mom would've wanted me to do this. It was a hollow consolation and made no impact on me. I don't know whether mom would've wanted me to do what I did. I don't know and frankly I don't care. I'd allowed myself to get into a situation where work had become too important. I did what I had to do and the fact that I had to do it was my fault.

What began on Sunday afternoon included seven cities, 25 meetings, and five full days. In the time between meetings, I sketched out my remarks for the funeral service, planned for Friday night. It was the hardest week of my life. Mom was gone, and I'd become something I didn't like.

As I arrived back in Knoxville on Friday evening, I was apprehensive and scared. I spent my career speaking publicly, was comfortable in the role, and rarely shied away from the opportunity. However, this was entirely different. I didn't want to do this, and I didn't want to be at the funeral home. Honestly, I was embarrassed, ashamed even. I felt the judgment of family and friends who knew I'd left mom and traveled across the country seeking investment dollars. No one said anything derogatory to me, and it may have all been my imagination, but I couldn't help it. I felt like a jerk.

After quickly navigating the entry hall filled with early arrivals, I shuffled into the chapel and immediately saw mom in her open casket lying before me. To me, she looked awful. Years of her struggle had turned her into a shell of herself, and she looked nothing like mom. To make matters worse, I noticed that her fingers were a translucent gray, as though she was beginning to decay, a process that should never be seen—only confined to a closed casket. I asked dad whether we could close the casket for the receiving of friends, and he said mom wanted that. I was relieved when the funeral director gently closed the lid.

Mom didn't deserve any of this. I'll never understand why this happened. It was pointless. A beautiful life had been taken. At that moment, years of watching her suffer and fight left me boiling inside, and I walked out of the side door, heading for the car. I just wanted to run away.

As mad as I was at myself and at what had happened to mom, I suddenly remembered what mom asked of me. She wanted me to do her eulogy, and she wanted it to be special. As if a robotic switch was flipped, I got focused and ready to share mom from my perspective with help from her.

Receiving friends is a strange tradition. The mourning family stands at the front of the church as attendees line up to pay their respects. People often struggle with what to say; it's awkward for everyone involved. It ends up being a repeating cycle of platitudes and "thanks for coming" responses. If the deceased was well-liked, the crowd could overwhelm the family. For mom, the line was long, and the process lasted for several hours.

For my wife and kids, many of the people who showed

up were unknown to them. It was almost unfair to expect them to stand there for the entire time, but they did. I was numb, but I wasn't alone. Mom's death wasn't a sudden tragedy; it was a drawn-out process that had become hard to watch. As such, the sense in the room wasn't emotionally charged, nor a celebration of life. It was a feeling of exhaustion.

Mom was loved and respected, her fighting spirit understood and admired by all. However, because of her final years with cancer, people had time to process her death on their terms. It's a strange thing to say, but the range of emotions ran the gamut. It reminded me of a funeral of a 90-year-old in which the most frequent refrain is that they lived a long, full life. Death seems easier to accept when life has been complete. We all die, and when a person has lived a long life, death seems to be the next step and is less painful. Even though mom was only 53, her death seemed like what was supposed to happen. Her struggle had been too much and had gone on for too long.

Mamaw was catatonic, but Xanax was getting her through. Dad was withdrawn and unable to be emotional. Rick handled the death with an odd mixture of humor and denial. I never understood how he processed things like this. It was foreign to me and created frustration. In hindsight, that's my fault. I somehow thought he should process things like I did. What a stupid notion. We're all different. I didn't take time to ask him about how he was feeling. Shame on me for being so about myself that I failed to recognize his pain.

To that point, I learned later that the day mom died, Rick had to go outside the hospital. He couldn't be there. He was obviously under major emotional stress, and fleeing was how he handled it. I respect that. I wish I'd been a better brother and spent private time with him to support his feelings. I wish I'd handled a lot of things better.

I don't remember a thing about the funeral service. Couldn't tell you who the pastor was, who else spoke at the service, or what was said. I don't even recall giving the eulogy. I wasn't feeling anything; I had just reached the point of blocking out the whole room. I built a wall to shield myself from everything and everyone. I was there, but I wasn't present.

As I began to think about this part of the book, I discovered that I had a copy of the eulogy I gave. I cried when I read it. Years of repressing the feelings I had about my own failures and shame exploded. I wasn't expecting that reaction, and it took me a few days to recover. Then I reread what I'd said. I did what mom wanted, and I think she would've approved.

She wanted me to remind people why she fought so hard, so that her grandkids would remember her, and they do. In fact, recently they were together, and the topic of nana's special white cake with orange icing came up. They loved the cake and swore it possessed a secret ingredient that they've yet to figure out as adults. Hoping they could finally understand what it was, they asked Aunt Karen to see whether she knew. Karen smiled. "Nana made those cakes using boxed cake mix and orange coloring for the icing. The special ingredient you guys remember was her love." All the grandkids nodded and agreed: That was a special additive that never could be replicated.

As I read the eulogy, I'm reminded that mom accepted that she lived long enough for the grandkids to know her, and how she wanted me to know what her final goal was. She said she had been searching for another challenge. I quoted her in my remarks. She said, "I've received a gift from God. A lot of people die quickly; it just happens. They're there one day and gone the next." She continued, "But I've been around. Most people know I'm dying, so what's my gift? My gift is I get to help people understand how to remember me. I get to help people understand who I am."

I don't remember internalizing this when she said it to me, nor when I repeated it at the service. Today, I get it. She lived to finish a task: to define herself to those around her. She did, and showed us that her attitude wasn't just a show. It thrived when she was experiencing the worst of times. Life is full of hard times, but mom showed us that you can make it through whatever you face.

She showed that toughness, tenderness, and humor can all exist together. She reminded me that being stubborn has its limits and its benefits. She reinforced her Christian spirit and faith. It would've been easy to grow mad at God, lose faith, or succumb to anger or bitterness. She never did.

She was faithful to her family and worried about us when all we wanted to do was worry about her. I used to joke that mom would get worried if she couldn't think of something to worry about.

I shared as many traits about mom as I could to the gathered congregation. I wanted her last purpose to be reinforced, but the truth is that her friends and family in the room knew. They knew her before cancer, and they watched her for seven years after the diagnosis. Thus, I didn't need to remind them. She did just fine delivering on her self-imposed promise.

I ended the eulogy with this thought: "At first glance, it feels like we have lost a lot with mom's passing, but the reality is that last Monday, we gained her back. We lost her body, but we have her presence. I'm happy to have her return to my consciousness without cancer and the daily misery it presented. I take solace knowing she isn't suffering. She's smiling and, if she can, is cooking. Mom was a special person. I'm proud of her. I know you're proud of her. She was proud of us."

Twenty-four years removed from that day, and older today than she was when she died, my love for her and pride in her life have only grown.

PART IV

# CHAPTER 16

DEATH IS A DIFFICULT CONCEPT. Based on what we know, humans are the most advanced life forms in existence. We're born with a mind, the ability to reason, contextualize, learn, feel, grow, love, hate, create, destroy, and think. We come into the world like most other living mammals, and we all die. Mathematically, humans are only alive for a tiny amount of time relative to the history of the world, and the planet contains billions of people. When you think about it, individuals seem so small in terms of time and numbers. We're each a little slice of a very big world, and yet, to us, our time on earth seems so full and comprehensive.

Because we have souls and can experience life on a deeper level, most of us invest heavily in our existence and, therefore, become inextricably bound to our loved ones. We generally exist within a community and feel the importance of belonging and the power of human connectivity. Whether that connection is family, friends, a significant other, or colleagues, people experience their time on earth enjoying others. Because we build deep emotional connections, losing a person to death is profoundly difficult. A part of our life is missing.

Death is bewildering to me. My mind struggles with the realization that it's over. I'll never see, speak to, hear, touch, or smell that person again. All that's left are memories, and hope that there's a promise that we'll reconnect.

I'm not going to lie: When mom died, I found little confidence in the belief that we'll meet again. I thought maybe we will, maybe we won't. It was then, and still is, unknowable. What I knew was that for as long as I breathed, mom would no longer be in my life.

After mom's passing, I became aware of people who talked about feeling the person they lost still being present in their lives, or that their souls were watching over them. I don't challenge that notion. Each person has their own feelings. It just wasn't my immediate experience.

For me, accepting mom as being present in my life wasn't possible until I found a way to heal myself. I needed to unpack the truth of mom's journey and allow myself to think of her without pain, anguish, or guilt.

I now know that I'm not alone in finding the finality of death to be overwhelming. For many, including me, a death opens the door to so many layers of emotions, like regret. I constantly asked myself what I could've done, should've done. I spent years finding examples of things that I wish I would've done differently. It's a feeling that can eat you up inside, and it did. It was a path to nowhere, I know, but I've spent years beating myself up.

As much as I've suffered from self-imposed shame for things I failed to do, nothing has bothered me as much as the number of things I don't know. When I think literally about death, I have way more questions than answers. In time, I've learned to accept that there's much that the living likely will never know, and I'm now OK with that.

I've come to recognize that not knowing is the very foundation of faith. A willingness to believe gives people the ability to march onward despite myriad unknowns that we face. Simply put, faith allows people to exist. That must be true. As rational, cognitive beings who are curious and always thinking, discovering that you never absolutely will know the answer leaves you with two options: Give up and not give a damn about anything, or accept faith in something bigger than you and choose not to worry about what's to come. Theologians have studied this, and I'm sure they have a better way to describe this evolution, but I'm not a theologian. I'm a normal guy who tries to find answers and make everything make sense. Death and the spiritual transition create so many questions for a critical thinker. Therefore, the answer must be, and has become for me, faith in the promise.

I still feel profound sadness when I lose someone in my life. I can't bring myself to say they're in a better place. All I can do is rely on my core belief that there must be a punchline to this story. Spirituality has been a part of the human journey since the beginning. It's so powerful because we want to believe––no, we must believe––in something bigger than the absoluteness of our meager existence on this planet.

Since mom's death, I lost my brother Rick. In the summer of 2012, he fell asleep on his couch and didn't wake up. He was 42. I'll never forget the moment dad called me and said, "Rick is gone."

So sudden and final. I could never speak to him again. I was asked after his passing whether we were close. I hate the question. We were brothers who grew apart, but his loss rocked me. Unlike mom's death, this was out of the blue. No one expects a healthy 42-year-old to die in their sleep. The event's suddenness meant there wouldn't be time for us to reestablish a deeper connection. Another death, more regrets.

I didn't understand why this happened, and to this day, I don't get it. Why does someone in good health, with so much left to do, depart this world? I hear people say it was God's plan. What kind of plan is this? He had three kids who still needed their dad. I don't get it, and I never will.

It was a blow for me, but it was a real dagger for dad. Losing a child is brutal, and he was close to Rick. They were so alike. Dad remarried, but he slowly was losing his nuclear family. His sadness never left him, and he called me each year on the anniversary of Rick's death. He missed him and his family.

I remember that when I saw Rick in the casket, I was floored. He didn't look peaceful, or like himself. He didn't look real. At this point, I hadn't worked through how

I felt about death. I couldn't process our life together. I only could feel deep sadness and fear. I don't know why, but for the first time, I saw myself lying in a casket. It was as though his sudden death jolted me back to a dark place I'd resided in after mom died.

My healing process began last year when I started to read and write about mom's diary. I was forced to stop and think about her final years and why I maintained such deep despair over the loss of a soul I loved. I was making daily progress working through her diary when tragedy struck. Dad fell, hit his head, and severely damaged his brain stem. He stopped breathing, was given CPR, and was kept alive as they flew him to Vanderbilt Hospital in Nashville. Diana, dad's wife, called and told me the details, and with that, we were in the car on our way to Nashville.

He was awake, but was paralyzed, couldn't speak, and was unable to breathe on his own. It was the saddest thing I've ever seen. His eyes looked scared. He blinked constantly and tried to mouth words. Nothing was decipherable. He was trying to say something, but couldn't. After a day, the doctors told us he wasn't going to recover and would never breathe without assistance.

Even though dad wasn't unconscious, there's no way he wanted this. Unfortunately, his living will didn't directly address this situation. It was left to Diana to decide what to do. She was heartbroken and sought input from me. It was a loving, respectful conversation that lasted for most of the day. On the second day, we agreed to remove the breathing tube.

Having to make this decision was harder than words can describe. It's the ultimate responsibility. We didn't want to say goodbye, and I'm sure dad didn't want to die. But I'm also certain he didn't want to spend months or years in a hospital bed unable to breathe or eat on his own. I think of the choice and his frightened face often. I doubt I'll ever get the look on his face out of my mind.

Diana, Tiffiny, Ryan (my stepbrother), and I sat quietly as the nurses prepared for what was to come. They slowly administered medication to allow him to rest. He looked peaceful. In time, the nurse came in and said they were going to remove the tube. She asked whether we wanted to step out for a moment or stay with him during her process. I immediately said I wanted to stay. I was holding his hand. He held my hand when I needed him, and it was the least I could do to hold his hand through this.

Dad's breathing slowed. He went peacefully shortly thereafter.

I put my hand on his chest and prayed for him. He was a good man who had provided for his family. Now he was gone too.

I immediately felt alone. My childhood family members all had died. Even though I have a wonderful wife and kids, I felt a loneliness that's indescribable. It was as though an entire segment of my life was known only by me. Whom could I relive the pre-college years with? There wasn't anyone remaining who ever would know the experiences from my nuclear family days or remember stories from our family life.

That feeling hasn't left me. I still feel alone in this

world. Today, I often think of my early days. This is new for me. For years, I've been so myopic about my life, my future, and what I'm doing now that I rarely revisited the days that made me who I am. I now find peace in reflecting on my formative years. I also find myself thinking of calling mom, dad, or Rick. Flashbacks to the past cause my mind to want to reach out to them. It's an instinctual reaction, then reality hits, and I'm reminded that I'm alone. I can't help it; I feel a mixture of comfort to have reconnected to my past and sadness when I think of all that was lost.

Since dad died, I've begun to do things that make me feel whole—little things that remind me of the joy my family brought me and the things we loved. I don't recall the moment I decided that this was important, and I didn't know that these traits were still in me. But they were, and they redefined me.

I've found joy in cooking; it connects me to mom. When I'm in the kitchen, I now feel her with me. We have fun. I've begun to focus on working in my garden. This was a passion for dad. He always worked in the yard. The other day, I was toiling away in the garden, and I felt so connected with dad. It was a special time.

My brother had the capacity to be friends with and friendly to everyone. As an introverted person, it always bothered me, but he was right: Personal interaction with people feeds the soul. When I find myself talking to someone who I might have dismissed before, I think of Rick.

Twenty-four years removed from mom's death, I now

can say I that understand the feeling that lost loved ones are with you. It's comforting and brings a smile to my face. They're not with me in body, and I still, and likely always will, feel alone, but I do sense their presence in my life.

At dad's funeral, I closed his eulogy with the following: "And now, dad, mom, and Rick are together, and someday, I'll join them."

I don't know why I believe that, but I do.

# CHAPTER 17

D ID MOM LIVE THE LIFE she wanted to live? It's a
question that haunted me after she died. It captured
my focus and never left my mind. I tried for years to gain
clarity, some deeper understanding of her true feelings
about the life she led, but was unable to reach any conclusions. Thus, over time, I started to rewrite secretly the
narrative on how I viewed her life and interpreted it. At
face value, it's an odd thing to wonder about a parent's
happiness. Whether or not mom lived her desired life
shouldn't have impacted me, but it did.

Truth be told, I was anxious to hear mom's private
voice shared in her diary to see whether I could discern
anything. I was certain that I'd learn she felt a sense of
longing, of lost opportunity, and maybe even disappointment. Once I began to read her words, things became
clearer, but not the way I'd imagined it.

To my surprise, I found nothing in mom's writing to convince me that she was unhappy with her life before cancer. It didn't take me long to conclude this. It also didn't take me long to recognize that my obsession with this subject wasn't about mom. It was about me.

When I look back on my life, career, and expectations for what I wanted to accomplish, a clear shift in me occurred after mom got cancer. I was 25 and I didn't recognize it at the time, but I began to drift away from my core being. I made professional choices that didn't fit my goals, interests, or true personality. I began to chase recognition, money, and prominence. I was trying to be something I'm not. I was trying to please others who, through no intentional fault of their own, projected an expectation onto me that I internalized and pursued.

I love my wife and would do anything and everything for her. She never asked me to evolve into a different person, but her family came from a different mindset, and whether or not they knew it, they had an expectation for me. It wasn't as though they forced me. They just failed to recognize that I was different from them. I wasn't motivated by the things they were. I experienced this disconnect when we were together. All conversations were through the prism of how they saw life. I felt completely out of place.

As a result, I decided I was going to seek and earn their approval. Like my mom, who sought to be a pleaser above almost anything else, I shared her need to please. What I didn't understand was that pleasing is best done when you're also serving yourself. Pleasing others while sacrificing your own self is destructive. For me, it led to bitterness, an anger that for the most part, I kept hidden and to myself. What I didn't keep unseen was a growing arrogance and abrasive nature that only served to mask my deep pain I felt for what I was doing, and how I was doing it.

Recently, I began to sense how far afield I had drifted. I reached an age when reflection was natural, and when I looked back at myself and stared into the mirror, I didn't like what I saw. It was, and is, hard to admit that most of what I've done professionally since mom got sick was an exercise in unhappiness. A cloud hung over me, and I struggled with what to do, if anything. I spoke with my Aunt Karen and shared some of my concerns about my past. I was seeking her thoughts, but steered away from the issues around my efforts to please my in-laws. I wasn't ready to admit the obvious to her. Nevertheless, just like mom, Karen says what she means and without hesitation, said, "Mike, you always tried to please your in-laws." She was right, and I knew if she saw it, it would be obvious to everyone from my past. She wasn't judging, just observing. I love her candor and willingness to say what mom would've said.

As my anxiety grew, I finally turned to mom's diary. I hoped, and expected, to hear mom reflect on her life and give me something to allow me to accept my wayward path and find peace. I wanted guidance from her writings.

And I got it. At some point in her diary, I started to remember mom as I knew her before cancer attacked her body. I recalled her strength and passion for life. I remembered that prior to cancer, she was my anchor. She never held me back, allowing me to be me, but did so by reminding me of where I came from and what I was about. When I got too big for my britches, she let me know, then hugged me. When I got pissy, she would say, "Mike, I know you're mad, but you got the same skin to get glad in."

Mom had the ability to do many things in her life. She was smart, talented, hardworking, and tough. She could've been more than a wife, mom, and administrative worker, but she didn't want more. She wanted what she had and relished it. She was happy working at the concession stand at the little league baseball park, cooking a mess of food for an army of hungry boys, or going to every sporting event that involved her favorite team. Her life wasn't perfect, but nothing is.

Before cancer, she was a guidepost for my life. I talked to her every day and always went to sleep with some reminder of who I was. Her disease took that from me. Gone was the lifeline to my past. I felt the void almost daily, until enough time passed that I forgot her wisdom, guidance, and even protection that allowed me to be OK being me.

I don't know whether my life would've turned out different if she had lived into her 70s. I think it would have, but it doesn't do any good to consider these possibilities. I can't change what happened to her, nor my actions. Truth be told, I'm not trying to rewrite my history. I've lived a blessed life and have accomplished many things.

Mom embraced her life, and I need to do the same. I need to return to who I am.

Mom spoke to me through her diary. It was sad, depressing, and hard to read, but I still found her true being through all the noise. I feel comfortable in saying that mom lived the life she wanted to live, and I feel equally confident saying I didn't. But today, I have enough of a reminder of mom to allow me to thrive as my true self. I'm making changes in my life—changes I wish I could tell her about.

The loss of my mom, dad, and brother has left me standing alone, but their memories are now fresh. I can see who I was and now who I want to be. Writing this has been helpful. I've struggled for a long time to understand my internal feelings. The time I spent with mom through her diary has given me a blessing. Like she did in my early years, she's now impacting how I view the world and, I believe, bringing me back to my true self.

# CHAPTER 18

Sometimes I overthink things. I seek to understand why things happen, and why people do what they do. It's a need to explore how people make decisions, what drives them, and how I might learn from their experience. It brings me peace to assume that someone is acting on their terms and of their own free will. Maybe if others can handle a situation, I can too. Admittedly, I'm biased. I want to believe we can handle anything if we're actively engaged in determining how we live. It's likely a naïve notion, and I know that, but I still hold onto the hope that more times than not, people who are emotionally in charge are better able to thrive. Unfortunately, it seems that humans tend to spend little time considering what's ahead and more time just doing whatever is in front of them. Sometimes blindly.

Mom fought tirelessly to beat cancer, enduring misery

and a substandard existence. It was impressive, but it didn't make sense to me. I wanted to place a deeper meaning to her fight. I sought some anchor that explained her choices. She frequently spoke of her objective to live so the grandkids would remember her. It sounded logical and foundational, but for some reason, I didn't buy it. I'm not being cold. I don't dispute her love for her family and her passion for nana's grandbabies. I just thought there must be something more.

Her diary doesn't directly address why mom fought so hard. Although there are recurring reminders of what she verbally communicated about her grandkids, the explanation still doesn't square with me, nor with her daily existence. I didn't believe then, and I don't believe now, that mom consciously thought through everything and decided she would fight to live for some defined purpose.

So, what was it? And why do I feel the need to know?

A terminal diagnosis forces someone to think about what comes next. Mom was Christian in belief and practice. To my knowledge, she never faltered, and I see no evidence in her writings that she doubted what was to come. She died believing she would be welcomed into heaven for eternity.

Believing in a higher being and that your loved one will be in peace is a comforting thought for those who remain and for those who are about to depart. For the faithful, it's the final chapter of their spiritual journey, but the promised passage into a "better place" created a lingering question in my mind that I couldn't reconcile.

If mom anticipated the gifts of heavenly eternity, why not accept her fate when the bone marrow transplant failed and pass more peacefully? She could've avoided the horrible, dreadful life she lived and died comfortably. She could've, but obviously didn't.

Mom wasn't afraid of dying and didn't dwell on what would happen to her after she died. She believed and accepted God's will. Her fight wasn't a fight against death and a deep-seated fear of the next chapter. Her need to fight was part of her being.

It seems clear today: Mom didn't know how to quit, and she'd never allow herself to disappoint others. It never occurred to her to consider anything but beating cancer. Every day, she found a way to get through the day, all with the hope that a miracle or cure for breast cancer would be discovered. She knew it wasn't likely to happen, but she fought on.

Mom came from tough stock. Her kin were gentle, loving, caring, and hardened. Estelle's family came from middle Tennessee and were decidedly poor. Tommy's family were natives of east Tennessee and the byproduct of hard Appalachian living. It's impossible for me to internalize the challenges they faced. Times were hard, opportunities were limited, and education was viewed as a luxury.

Immediately following the Civil War, families in the South struggled. Reconstruction didn't help, and the Great Depression drove a struggling rural population into a life of subsistence. And yet, they endured. They did what they had to do. They didn't have time to plan their future. There were kids to feed, work to be done, and daily tasks that couldn't be delayed.

Mom was born when opportunities were expanding in the South. She was the first generation in her family unit that didn't have to wonder whether a high school education was possible. She was a baby boomer and the beneficiary of the developing middle class after World War II. Nevertheless, as a child, mom was poor. She watched her parents struggle to provide a better future for her. She understood her family's history and what it meant to work hard. She saw firsthand the obstacles that life brings you. She was a doer. She was born and raised that way.

Mom dealt with cancer like she did every other challenge. She fought every day and didn't need some higher purpose. She couldn't/wouldn't give up. It never seemed to cross her mind. Her perseverance is humbling for me.

After all my professional years, I think of myself as well-read and thoughtful. I operate under some false sense of understanding of how people live. How could I have missed the truth about mom? She didn't view her cancer fight through my glasses. She accepted cancer like everyone else in her life accepted bad stuff. It was another part of living, and she was going to get on with living.

My newfound awareness of what was really going on with mom adds to my respect for her. I now realize I don't need to discover whether mom had some grand purpose. She didn't need it, and that's good enough for me. She ended her life like she lived it: doing the best she could to please, and fighting when times were hard.

Years ago, as part of a retreat, I was asked if I could ask my mom one question, what would it be. Without hesitation, I responded, "I'd ask her if it was all worth it?"

That question once lingered in my mind. Today, I wonder why that was so important to me. It's antithetical to all that mom taught me. "No need to look back and find regrets; can't change things, so why worry about it?" she would say.

The very notion of "Was it worth it?" screams of a self-loathing pity party covering seven years. She would've hated the inquiry and been annoyed beyond belief had I brought that question to the table as my one last chance to seek her counsel.

She would be right. It's a silly question, and I'm glad to have cast it out of my mind. It doesn't matter whether it was worth it. She fought cancer and lived longer than she was supposed to live. She accomplished, or didn't accomplish, whatever she wanted, and I'm in no position to wonder whether it was worth what it cost her.

My freedom from this nagging unknown about mom's journey, and the barriers it built inside me, has allowed me to understand what's really impacting me. My prior need to explore whether mom had regrets isn't about her. It's about my deeply held disappointment in me and how I remember my actions.

# CHAPTER 19

I NEVER SHOULD'VE LEFT HER BEDSIDE. It was stupid, and my single greatest failure. I know what people have said––mom would've wanted me to do what I needed to do. To this day, when the subject comes up, it's the standard retort––and it's bullshit.

Today, I can't tell you what I gained from putting my business before my family. The transaction was successful, but who cares? I can't remember one name of the handlers who made the trip with me, nor the investment bankers. I couldn't give you a rundown of any investors who committed that week. I was performing a task that seemed critical. I thought it was vital, in that moment, like everything else is. However, it turned out to be another self-created crisis that consumed me. If I hadn't gone on that trip, it wouldn't have altered one thing about my professional life. Not one damn thing.

Not staying with mom impacted me. It has been a recurring memory that brings me private shame. How could I have drifted so far from my core beliefs to think that putting nameless, greedy investors ahead of mom was even an option?

I've spent countless hours trying to reconcile my decision, and I know that this obsession with why I did what I did is counterproductive. Frankly, the self-reflection hasn't yielded any insights that make me feel better. It's a vicious cycle that has created recurring anxiety. Until recently, I haven't been able to shake this dark moment.

I think my departure from the hospital in the final few hours that mom was alive reflected how my life had evolved since she got cancer. Our relationship wasn't the same, and a void formed. Work, personal ambitions, and the need to please others filled the gap. By the time mom died, my relationship with her had become detached. On some level, the disconnect was due to my inability to watch her fade. I couldn't stomach it, as it didn't fit my view of her. She always solved my problems for me, and now I couldn't solve her crisis. On another level, I'd become self-absorbed and a little full of myself. I was doing big things and thought I was becoming a big shot.

I also was lonely. I knew that I was changing, and when I was honest with myself and wanted to slow down and get back to my roots, I ultimately was unwilling. I still harbored some awareness of my internal conflict, so I was keenly aware of how detached I'd become from mom and her fight. My understanding of what I was doing gnawed at me and was a constant conflict. I just didn't feel shame in her final hours of life, and I felt that way for years. The last act was inevitable and the culmination of years of guilt. I hadn't lived up to what I should've done, and I felt like mom, and everyone knew it.

In time, and with the help of this project, I've learned to think of this experience differently. I'll never accept my failure that weekend in November, 1999. I won't let that go; I don't want to forget it. However, I've learned to forgive myself. I don't believe that mom would've wanted me to leave, but I know she would've wanted me to forgive myself. I made a mistake, but I can't change that. It need not haunt me. We all try to do the best we can. I failed at this, and my acceptance of that truth has enabled me to be more vulnerable, humble, and comfortable in my own skin. Life is hard, but it doesn't have to be overthought. At the end of the day, prioritizing what and how you do things is far more important than perfection.

I was far from perfect during the years mom was sick. I could spend days thinking of all that was lost, all I did wrong—all the regrets. I'm not doing that anymore. I've forgiven myself.

# CHAPTER 20

I DON'T KNOW WHAT I EXPECTED when I began to read mom's diary. It was uncharted territory, and I never read anything that mom previously had written. This would be a new data point. Maybe I'd experience additional insight into who she was and how she thought. The optimist in me was eager to learn something positive and change the narrative I had in my head.

However, there was another side to this. I was very apprehensive about reading the diary. Her seven-year struggle always provided the saddest of memories. Maybe this would add to it and only deepen my internal demons. More likely, I was terrified it would open closely guarded personal wounds. I approached the pages of her diary a broken person. What if the experience was more than I could handle? What if I couldn't rise out of my isolated misery?

I tried to consider the pros and cons that could result from reading her personal thoughts. My thoughts weren't organized, I was acting without my normal guardrails, and I was full of anxiety. Then one day, I sat down and began to read and write. It was time. I'd reached a point in my life when my personal happiness was at an all-time low, and I needed to find a way out of the hole I was in.

I remember the first day. All I accomplished was reading the first entry. I didn't write a thing. I read the paragraph and sat silently for a long time. The drain from the initial attempt left me wondering whether I could process this. I placed the diary down on my desk and walked away. Fortunately, the next morning, I was looking forward to taking the first step of my journey. Without any emotion, I wrote the introduction.

Reading and writing about mom's life, struggles, vulnerabilities, and challenges was tough. There were many days when reading an entry led to a flood of tears. Sometimes the tears were because of mom's words, other times an entry elicited a painful memory, and sometimes an entry spoke directly to me and stopped me in my tracks. During the first phase of mom's diary, my sadness was directed exclusively toward mom. I was reminded of how tenuous life can be. She was healthy, living her best life, and it was stripped away. Remembering the early days led to emotional pain and a new layer of mourning. Interestingly, as the diary progressed, and the cancer returned, my thoughts shifted from sadness about mom to a deeper assessment of what was happening with her and those around her. Specifically, my thoughts and writing evolved to focus on my personal memories, regrets, and guilt.

Honestly, I initially thought I was writing about mom, her diary, and her story. Turns out, this was also about me. I couldn't separate the two. Mom had cancer, she fought valiantly, and she taught all of us about perseverance. As she fought to live, I became a different person. After her death, I couldn't figure out how to work my way back to who I wanted to be. This diary did that for me. It was as if I was talking to mom every day, just like before. There were tears, laughter, tough love, peaceful moments, questions, answers, guidance, and an unending connectivity. She was no longer alive in a human form, but was alive in my heart, mind, and soul.

It took 30 years detached from mom for me to become lost. It took a year with her diary to find myself.

I'm now more aware that my feelings, or some form of them, are not the exception. As I invested more time in this, I've learned to engage with others about their losses and struggles. What I've seen reinforces a belief that I have: The world is hard, and we're imperfect beings. We possess the ability to do great things and dumb things, make mistakes, redeem ourselves, hurt and love others, and grow. My takeaway: It's OK to accept ourselves for who we are. We were made to be imperfect. We need not have all the answers, which is good because we don't have all the answers.

Death is still a mystery to me. This experience didn't give me some brilliant, new insight. I still don't know how to process permanent loss, and I'm OK with that.

Mom, dad, and Rick are gone, but they're still with me, and I'm with them.

I'm also with my nuclear family. I've found a different peace with Tiffiny and our two fabulous kids. They grew up and witnessed my personal pain. Kids are smart. They may not have known what was affecting me, but I'm sure they knew something was. They certainly view me differently now. I feel blessed to have found this renewed approach while we have time together.

I'm sad that this project is almost completed. I found strength from my daily attention to this diary and book. I'm more at peace than I've been in a long time. Life feels better.

I have a new grandchild. He is, of course, adorable. I look at him with a love I've never felt. There's an unexplainable sense of pride, as well as a feeling that I'm my family's elder statesman. No longer am I a child in a larger group. I'm the senior person in my family. It's not a bad thing. It's as if the torch has been passed.

Mom once told me, "Even when you're 50, you'll still be my baby." I'm OK with that. I wish she was here to say that and to hold my grandbaby. Since she can't, every time I hold him, I give him a little kiss from nana.

I wanted to honor mom when I wrote about her. I hope I have. She was a special person who impacted many lives. Like all of us, she wasn't perfect, but I think that makes her all the more human. Life is joyous, and it's hard. It's meant to be that way.

Mom was real, as was her cancer fight, and the love she shared with all who touched her was real. Today, when I think of mom and tears well up, they're tears of happiness. She's infused in my soul, and all that she offered I intend to honor with those I love and know. I can't thank her enough for the gift of life and the spirit to embrace each day.

Mom, I'm back. Until we meet again....

# Acknowledgements

L IFE IS A MEANDERING JOURNEY shared with many people––some impactful, others not so much. I'm blessed to have been surrounded by friends and family who witnessed my behavior and likely wondered why I seemed unsettled. I didn't allow others to see my internal struggles, and yet, they never quit on me. I'm profoundly appreciative of those who cared for me and made my life better. At the top of that list is my wife, Tiffiny, my best friend and life partner who supported all my crazy ideas and activities, and never blinked. She gave birth to two wonderful kids and provided an environment of love and laughter. As my former coach says, "I outkicked my coverage." Thanks, also, to Ashley and Thomas. Words cannot adequately express how proud of them I am, nor how much I admire whom they've become. As they've grown, they've demonstrated a special understanding and support of me. I value their love and friendship, and work every day to show them how much I love them.

Writing this wasn't easy. As I progressed through the diary, I sought help from Aunt Karen and Aunt Pam. I know they were a bit reluctant to revisit this painful memory, and I know they have doubts about me sharing this story. Nevertheless, they were engaged and willing to help in any way they could. They trusted and supported me. I'll be forever grateful.

I'm blessed to work with a special person who brings value and joy to me every day. Always smiling and ready to get things done, Ashley Fields has made my life better. Beyond this book, she supports me daily. I couldn't get much done without her.

A special thanks to my friends who encouraged and counseled me—Colin Martin, George Hashbarger, Sally Allen, Bill Mayer, Kevin O'Brien, Mike Semack, and Tom Flannery.

I appreciate your time and friendship.

## ABOUT THE AUTHOR

Michael was born in Knoxville, Tennessee. A lifelong lover of all things East Tennessee, he spent 30 years living all over the South. For the past 25 years, Michael has served as chief executive officer of numerous companies—some successful, others not. Along the way, he's been blessed to experience events and interact with thoughtful leaders who have impacted his life and made him wonder how this happened to the son of Pat and Ray. Today, Michael is executive chairman of Lirio, an AI company focusing on patient engagement in healthcare. Despite his travels and wide-ranging career, Michael never emotionally is far from home. In expectation of many grandkids, he now lives in Bristol, Tennessee, with his wife of 35 years, Tiffiny. They have two children. Ashley and her husband Gautum live in Knoxville, Tennessee, and Thomas and his wife Alexa, and their almost-perfect son Emmett, live in Charlottesville, Virginia.